The Ten Commandments

of DATING

The Ten Commandments

of DATING

BEN YOUNG
& SAM ADAMS

THOMAS NELSON PUBLISHERS
Nashville

Published in Nashville, Tennessee, by Thomas Nelson, Inc., Publishers.

Scripture quotations are from the HOLY BIBLE: NEW INTERNATIONAL VERSION ®. Copyright © 1973, 1978, 1984 by International Bible Society. Used by permission of Zondervan Publishing House. All rights reserved.

Names and Stories in this book are based on actual incidents. However, all names and details have been changed to protect privacy.

Library of Congress Cataloging-in-Publication Data

Young, Ben.
    The ten commandments of dating / Ben Young & Sam Adams.
        p.   cm.
    Includes bibliographical references.
    ISBN 0-7852-7022-1 (pbk.)
    1. Dating (Social customs) 2. Dating (Social customs)—Religious aspects—Christianity. I. Adams, Sam. II. Title.
HQ801.Y68 1999
646.7'7—dc21   98-47789
                                                                                                    CIP

Printed in the United States of America
8 9 10 11 12 13 14 15 – 04 03 02 01

to eLLIott
aND JULIe

Contents

Acknowledgments

The authors would like to thank friends, family members, and coworkers for their support and encouragement along the way. We are especially thankful to Julie Adams and Elliott Young, who gave us a basis for understanding true love and commitment.

Many thanks to the team at Thomas Nelson including Mike Hyatt, Cindy Blades, and Kathy Wills.

Thanks also to Mark Boswell, Tom Thompson, and Sealy Yates for their wisdom and guidance. Special thanks to Glenn Lucke, Kiersten Berry, and Suzanne Penuel for their expertise and valuable input.

And finally to all those who participated in the process of making this book a reality: Jody Hatt, Gena Strader, and Laura Wright for their wonderful attitudes, organizational skills, and continuous support; Dave Riggle (the greatest "shallow psychologist" in the world); Leigh McLeroy for her invaluable feedback; Charlie Davis and the entire crew at Winning Walk; Mike Morrison for his incredible engineering skills at the Single Connection; Dr. Jim Rolf for planting the original seed for this book years ago; and Robert Nagel, Spencer Hayes, Jim Kemper, Jeff Riddle, and Darroll Paiga (The Austin Mens' Friday Group).

Introduction

If you are like most singles, you are tired of the dating scene. You are tired of pouring time, energy, and money into relationships that start off great and end with heartache. Maybe you are frustrated because you can't find The One for you, no matter how hard you pray, primp, and plead. Maybe you've been in many serious relationships, but for some unknown reason you can't seem to close the deal. Or perhaps you are single again and are afraid of making the same mistakes that resulted in so much pain and disillusionment in previous relationships.

While I (Ben) can't "feel your pain," I can definitely relate. There were times in my dating career that I felt so confused and put out with the whole system, I thought my brain would explode. I said, "God, either arrange a marriage for me or make me a monk, because this dating thing ain't working." I was so disillusioned that Mother Teresa's way of life looked more attractive than ever.

During my dating struggle, I began to write down quips and theories (like "The Platonic Relationship Theory," "The Heisman Trophy Treatment," and "The Heavy Metal Headbanger Trap") to teenagers, college students, and singles. After a few years, I coined nearly fifty dating terms, a collection we call "Swami Ben's Theories and Observations on the Mixed-Up, Crazy World of Relationships." Granted, I was no relationship swami, but through experience and a lot of thought, I was learning the basics on how to make the dating thing really work.

Finally, the dating thing worked in my life, and not just in my theories. God did not answer my bogus prayer request to arrange a marriage or turn me into a monk, but He did allow me to meet the woman of my dreams, learn how to grow in this relationship, and eventually get married. Finding such a woman was well worth the years of pain, struggle, and loneliness.

During a decade of working with thousands of singles, and gleaning wisdom from my own dating experiences, I began to discover not just relationship theories, but relationship laws. In other words, there were laws of dating just as there were laws of nature. I noticed that if you kept these laws—we call them commandments—you would be blessed, and if you broke them you would be cursed. I called my good friend, clinical psychologist, Dr. Sam Adams, to see if these laws I observed were based in reality or if I was just delusional. He verified that I was not insane, and told me he also believed there were some absolutes in the dating process. We decided to combine my street-smart insights and observations of relationships with his clinical knowledge and counseling expertise, and this book is the result.

OUR VISION

Our vision in writing this book is to provide you with ten time-tested relationship laws to protect you from the pitfalls of modern dating, and greatly increase your odds of successful dating. We promise to stay away from contemporary, relativistic dating theories. Our goal is not to tickle your ears or fill your mind with pseudopsychological platitudes on relationships. There is enough bad advice on dating being spewed out on TV sitcoms and talk shows to fill legions of singles bars and health clubs. This book will give you practical, no-nonsense commandments on how to make dating work (and please don't be offended by our political incorrectness). Keep in mind, these are not suggestions or recommendations based upon surveys and opinion polls. These are solid "truths" that, for the most part, have a moral foundation. If you keep the Ten Commandments of Dating, your relationships will run more smoothly, you will protect yourself from the pain of contemporary dating pitfalls, and you will be on your way to building loving, lasting relationships.

Having said that, we want to acknowledge two attitudes that often bring about resistance to the idea of nonnegotiable laws for dating (we may as well address them up front):

1. Moral Relativism

One of the most disturbing trends in our society is the attitude of moral relativism (especially rampant among Generation Xers). The essence of this belief is that there are no absolute truths, all truth is relative. Therefore, what's true for you may not be true for me, according to this approach. Moral relativists stress "tolerance" and what "feels right." They do not believe in an absolute standard that helps distinguish between clear right and wrong. In fact, they are offended by this idea. Because this attitude is so pervasive in our culture, you can't help but be influenced by it somewhat.

Are there absolutes? Do we have a source for truth? We believe the answer is a resounding *yes*. Call us old-fashioned if you will, but we believe that the Bible has a lot more to say about successful relationships (directly and indirectly) than most people realize. And, we have no problem accepting it as the ultimate authority and standard for all time. We don't buy in to moral relativism, and we hope you don't either.

2. The Mystery of Relationships

The second attitude that often gets in the way of nonnegotiable laws of relationships is associated with the mysterious nature of relationships. Granted, there is a certain mystery and complexity to any type of relationship. There is something about love and attraction that is difficult to explain, and we readily agree that you can't just reduce successful relationships down to simple logic. Often, there are deeper needs and unconscious drives that influence our choices of dating partners. The temptation that many face is to concede to the mystery of relationships, throwing up their hands, and hoping for the best. We believe that you can do better than that. While we cannot and do not guarantee 100-percent success through some simple formulas, we do believe you can improve your chances, and help ensure a solid foundation for a good marriage in spite of the mystery. We also believe we have truth on our side—something that many feel-good, relationship experts cannot assert.

YOU'VE GOT NOTHING TO LOSE

We want to challenge you to seriously consider these laws. We suspect that much of your dating confusion can be eliminated if you simply keep these ten relational commandments. Remember, God gave Israel the Ten Commandments to show them how to live life. These ten are designed to show you how to succeed in your love life. Each chapter will spell out the benefits of keeping a commandment and the consequences of breaking it. If you've already broken a few, don't panic. You can follow the commandment and get back on track. It's never too late.

Dating is one of the most important processes you will ever go through, and it potentially can lead to one of the most important decisions of your life. YOU CAN'T AFFORD TO IGNORE THE LAWS IN THIS BOOK. This book is written from a Christian perspective. But you don't have to be a Christian for these laws to work for you. They still reflect truth. Regardless of your beliefs, when you respect these laws, you will be better off. When you violate the laws, you will experience negative consequences. If you have already glanced at our ten commandments and feel it's too late for you, relax. You are not alone. Negative consequences from poor choices may remain, but the good news is, it's never too late to start doing the right thing. Relationships will always be a mixed bag of joy and heartache, fun and serious work. Sure, dating is risky business—but doing it right is well worth the risk. We believe that if you keep these commandments, you will experience a greater depth of peace, love, and fulfillment in your own life and in your relationships. You have everything to gain, and nothing to lose.

THOU SHALT
GET A LIFE

It's 5:30 on a Friday afternoon, and you've just put in another forty-hour work week. You grab a Twinkie and a Coke, and plop down on your couch with the remote in one hand and your mail in the other. Shuffling through the junk mail, you discover that Ed McMahon has just made you a millionaire for the fifteenth time when you suddenly notice a letter from your sweetheart of more than a year.

You rip open the envelope, and dive into the letter. The words, *"I Don't Think We Should See Each Other Anymore"* explode off the page and fling themselves into your heart like pieces of hot shrapnel. This is a letter bomb, not a love note! Your heart sinks into your stomach as you realize that this person in whom you've invested so much time, energy, and emotion has just put an end to something you hoped would last forever. After you get over the initial shock, you check your answering machine to see if there is a message from your sweetheart about reconsidering—or at least something to ease the blow. Nothing. You feel deeply hurt, rejected, and all alone.

Several months pass, and for some strange reason things aren't getting any better. In fact, you are still stuck in the same emotional ditch you fell into the day you got your letter. As you continue to work through the pain, you replay the relationship in your head over and over. You ask yourself, "What went wrong? Who's to blame? Why did such a good thing go sour?"

Finally, a startling truth begins to emerge, and you realize why this relationship fizzled: you simply did not have a life. *This person* was your life. Your entire self-worth was wrapped up in someone else. You now see how you had put your life on hold—your career, interests, friends, and even your relationship with God. Thus, you had little to give to the relationship. Since the relationship has ended, you have nothing to sustain you. Without your sweetheart, you have no life.

Sadly, we have witnessed far too many scenarios just like the above illustration. Thousands of singles booby-trap their relationships or never even begin them in the first place because they ignore this first and foundational love commandment: Thou Shalt Get a Life!

Years ago the woman of my (Ben's) dreams dumped me twice within a six-week period. Although it felt like she had torn my heart right out of my rib cage, it turned out to be one of the most valuable experiences of my dating life. It was through that double dumping that I learned that the most important thing a person could bring to a relationship was a life. A *real* life! When you invest all your energy and self-esteem in getting a date or having a relationship, you don't have a life.

People with lives are not sitting around waiting to be swept off their feet. People with lives do not make "getting married" their ultimate goal. People with lives do not always have to be in a relationship or on a date to feel good about themselves. People with lives are not church-hopping, barhopping, or consulting phone psychics in hopes of finding The One. Relationships and marriage are important goals (why else would you be reading this book?), but they must be kept in perspective. When romantic relationships become an obsession or they are elevated to prime importance, you've got a problem.

Here's some sobering news: if you don't have a life of your own, you won't be happy even if you date, fall in love, and get married. Why? Because you will have nothing to give to the relationship, and you will drain your dating partner (or spouse) completely dry. Inevitably, you will put extraordinary expectations on the other to fulfill you, complete you, entertain you, and soothe you. No created thing—certainly no human—can perform up to those outlandish expectations. Only the Creator who made you can do that, and He made you to . . . get a life!

Before you ever go out again or say "I do," please follow this first and greatest commandment to Get a Life. If you are wondering what a real life looks like or how to get one, read on. But first let's see what can happen when someone decides to rebel and break this first law of relationships. We call it the un-life.

THE UN-LIFE

People who are living the un-life have one thing in common: they have put their lives on hold. They have become so consumed with finding someone to meet their needs and give them a sense of significance that real living has taken a backseat. Some un-lifers just withdraw completely and give up.

They have convinced themselves that life isn't worth pursuing with any sort of passion without a partner. Whether they are obsessed with finding The One or they have given up, these are the ones who have contracted the fatal disease of the un-life. Here are the most common symptoms of the un-life, known as the four Deadly Ds.

1. Desperation

A desperate person has a sense of urgency about finding a mate. He is starving for someone to fill the emotional hole in his soul. I (Sam) will never forget Mike, a very successful thirty-two-year-old real estate broker who had come to see me because he had recognized that he was running off women right and left. We soon discovered that part of his problem was his tendency to try and close the deal by the third date as if it were some kind of real estate transaction. His urgent need to fill a void kept him from going slower in order to allow a more normal, natural process of bonding to occur. Mike had a lot of assets, including money, prestige, and good looks, but he did not have the inner strength necessary to stave off his desperation. Mike eventually learned to slow down but only after he had deliberately invested time and energy into filling that void. He changed his priorities, and became a more balanced person with other passions in life.

Desperate daters are sometimes found lurking around certain milestones, such as graduation from college, a fortieth birthday, or wet ink on divorce papers. Unfortunately, their urge-to-merge strategy scares off potential mates instead of attracting them. Take some advice from Confucius: "Desperation produces perspiration and perspiration stinks on anybody."

2. Dependence

A dependent person gains a sense of significance and security through others. He must be attached to someone in order to feel good about himself. We've seen countless men and women hang on to sick relationships, even emotionally and physically abusive relationships, for this very reason. Kristen called Ben's radio show, *The Single Connection*, one night to discuss her relationship with Carl; she was separated from him, and seemed to be unable to make decisions for herself without him. To top it off, she confessed that Carl was aggressive and violent toward her and was thrown into prison as a result. He was to be released that weekend. Unbelievable as it may seem, she called the show to ask, "What should I do?" We have tremendous compassion for people like Kristen and we hold out much hope for those who acknowledge their difficulty and seek help.

Dependent daters have difficulty making decisions and taking responsibility for their lives and their own decisions. When a dependent person enters a relationship, he usually sucks the lifeblood out of the other person, like a tick on a dog. Two dependent daters face an even more impossible situation: two ticks, no dog! Of course, as humans we all depend on others to some degree for certain needs. This is normal and healthy. But a person infected with the un-life will be excessively dependent on the other person to meet most of his or her needs and provide a sense of identity.

3. Depression and Loneliness

Feelings of depression and loneliness are the number one complaint of singles who buy into the notion that someone else can make them happy. This can take many forms, but generally it is a condition that affects the whole person: physically, emotionally, and spiritually. Most people living the un-life will experience some feelings of depression, which may include such characteristics as unhappiness, gloom, lack of energy, and withdrawal from others. It is also not uncommon to experience a drop in self-confidence or self-esteem.

Reggie attempted to begin a relationship with several different women, and things just didn't click. After three failures and steeped in loneliness, Reggie began to lash out verbally at the women in conversation with his small circle of friends. Immersing himself more and more in the Internet, Reggie cut off normal connections with his peers and turned his room into a cave. Rage and distorted views of reality ensued, so that when Reggie made an occasional step back into the real world, he was a social black hole and even fewer people wanted to be around him. This only worsened the condition, and soon his life consisted mostly of surfing the Internet and watching television. Reggie exploded on his remaining friends, and he sank deeper into the abyss.

The danger in depression and loneliness is that it may begin a downward spiral. In other words, the more depressed you feel, the more likely you are to withdraw and further exacerbate the depression. Eventually, this can even lead to a more severe form of depression (clinical depression), which can involve symptoms such as loss of appetite and sleep, difficulty with concentration, problems with normal functioning, and feelings of hopelessness. This more severe form of depression calls for professional intervention such as counseling or therapy, and possibly medication.

The good news is that even in the downward spiral a person can be treated and begin a reverse spiral back to having a life. Reggie, after a violent episode, was directed toward a counselor. It took time, but eventually Reggie became a delightful person who cultivated numerous healthy relationships with folks who sought out his company. The un-life discarded, Reggie now experiences the fruits of having a real life in which he brings joy to those around him.

4. Detachment

"Isolated," "withdrawn," "lonely," and "watches the Jerry Springer show" describe someone who has disengaged from life. This person has detached himself from vital social relationships; the desire to spend time with friends, get involved in the community, or serve in a local church has vanished.

Linda, a vivacious woman in her early twenties was one of the most outgoing people you could ever meet. However, after a series of hurtful relationships, she began to withdraw to protect herself. Unfortunately, her well-intentioned plan backfired. Linda gained a lot of weight (which she admitted was a defensive, self-destructive move), sabotaged old friendships, and distanced herself from family members. In short order, Linda completely isolated herself from others. I'm sure Linda did not intentionally set out to withdraw so completely, and yet it can be easy for anyone to do once they start down this path.

Coping with the Un-Life: Media-Bation

In our high-tech society today, one of the biggest dangers for un-lifers is the tendency to use certain forms of media to cope with the isolation. This is what we call *media-bation*. People who look to the media as their primary (or only) source for meeting emotional and relational needs definitely need to get a life. They rely upon the television, radio, video, or Internet for fulfillment. Media-bators spend all their time in front of a screen, at Blockbuster, in a chat room, or at the local CD exchange. A vast subculture has arisen in which these folks can hide out. Recently, we were in a computer store purchasing software. We were blown away by the sheer number and variety of software and hardware gadgets, games, and joysticks—all the tools used by media-bators to escape life into the un-life of perpetual cyberdistraction.

At some point, all of us have descended into the un-life. The good news is that you don't need to call a doctor or go to a Benny Hinn Miracle Crusade to be healed from the un-life. If the four Ds describe you, then the way to a passionate, fulfilling life is through the antidote of the five Gs: You must become *grounded, grouped, goal-oriented, giving,* and *growing.*

How to Get a Life

1. Get Grounded

Getting grounded is the foundation for getting a life. It is all about having a solid identity and sense of self. This includes everything from recognizing one's worth and value to feeling self-confident and secure. Individuals with a solid identity can't be shaken or destroyed by dateless droughts or unceasing wedding invitations in the mail. They know who they are. They are complete and whole within themselves.

The dominant view in our society is that human worth, value, and happiness are obtained through tangible achievement and performance: if you have money, power, prestige, good looks, and intelligence, *then* you have worth. The message is, "The more you have, the greater your self-esteem." This formula can literally ruin your life.

Judging by this arbitrary standard, entertainment figures,

such as Michael Jackson, should be the most centered, self-confident, grounded people on this planet. He has talent, money, power, and millions of fans who love and worship him. What a tragedy it is to watch this "man-child" change his nose, lips, hair, and skin in an attempt to feel better about himself. In one sense, he has it all, but on the other hand, the King of Pop has nothing. He doesn't know who he is. He is not grounded.

Many of us are like Michael Jackson (though I hope your best friend isn't a chimp). We are busy working on the externals—our hair, face, body, clothes, possessions, and career—to give us a sense of self-worth. It's like putting a small band-aid over a huge wound.

I (Sam) counseled a young lady recently who seemed to have it all: great looks, stylish clothes, a new Lexus, her own business, and a wealthy, handsome man to boot. Yet, she was miserable and lonely. Why? *She had focused on the externals to try to fix the internals.* There is nothing wrong with working out, dressing well, and pursuing a career, but if you look only to those things to give you a sense of self-worth, you'll *always* be searching.

Self-worth is not something you go out and get. Self-worth is not something you buy, achieve, or obtain. It's something you *already* have. Getting grounded means embracing the fact that you are created in the image of God, and have *inherent* worth and value. This value is unchanging and complete. It's not something you can get more or less of depending on your achievements. Worth, based on being an image of God, does not fluctuate. This intrinsic worth does not change regardless of your personality, performance, or possessions, because it's based on the immutable character of God.

Think of it this way: God Himself made you, and He made

you *in His image*. That is, we are stamped with His image. We speak of money as coming in different denominations such as a dime, a quarter, a $5 bill, or a $100 bill. Each coin or bill has two things: an imprint of an image (like George Washington or Abraham Lincoln) and a specified value. A quarter is stamped with the image of George Washington and is worth 25 cents. You are denominated by God's name, you are stamped with His image, and thus your "coin" is of priceless value. Can you put a price on the value of God Almighty? No, and since you are stamped with the image of the Priceless One, you also are priceless. That is self-worth. Accepting this is the key to being grounded.

In light of this reality, Dr. Peter Kreeft, in *Knowing the God Who Loves You*, says,

> Accept yourself. Love yourself. Respect yourself. This is good advice properly understood. But why should I accept myself if I don't feel like it? What is the rock-solid, inescapable objective foundation for my self-love? If it is only my feelings or perceptions or my psychologist's perceptions, then my house of self-esteem is built on sand. When the rains come, my house of self-esteem will fall and it will be a cataclysmic fall. But if my house is based on God's Word, then even when the rains of bad feelings and self-doubt come, my house of self-esteem will stand firm because it is built on the rock of God's unchanging truth, not my ever shifting feelings about myself. Self-esteem is necessary for all psychological health, and there is no absolutely sure basis for self-esteem other than the assurance of God's love for me.[1]

When you see yourself the way God sees you, you will be free from insecurity and fear. What you believe about yourself and your core identity determines how you behave. Getting grounded is ultimately about being established in the rock-hard reality of God's love and favor to you.

2. Get Grouped

Psychologists say that one of our deepest needs is to be connected with others in a meaningful way. You were created by God with the desire to be in relationships with other people, and when this God-given desire goes unmet, you will suffer. You will experience an emptiness and longing that can only be filled when you are associated with others. *Getting grouped is all about developing replenishing relationships.* It is being involved with others beyond superficiality. It is about being in deeper relationships where there is trust, safety, and vulnerability.

Seinfeld, one of the top-rated TV shows in America for the past several years, was successful partially due to the series' emphasis on relationships and getting grouped. The characters on the show—Jerry, George, Elaine, and Kramer—were all singles living in New York City. In a strange way, these characters formed a type of family, giving each other support and encouragement (in a backhanded sort of way) as they faced life's daily struggles.

In our experience, we don't think it is a coincidence that the men and women who are passionate about life, God, and making a difference in the world are always involved in some sort of group. It may be an accountability group, Bible study, or some sort of support group, but the bottom line is that they are connected with others on a deep level. You are not an island or a Lone Ranger. You were designed for community.

Are you committed to a local church? Are you part of an accountability group or support group? Are you a member of a sports team? Do you participate in community service projects?

Do you have people in your life who encourage you and, when necessary, graciously confront you? Are you part of a group in which you listen to each other over time and reveal your deepest concerns? If not, take this step today. Inquire about joining or starting a group, and this will help propel you out of the unlife into having a vibrant life.

3. Get Goal-Oriented

A recent poll revealed that 27 percent of our population received some type of welfare, 60 percent were just getting by, 10 percent were considered moderately successful, and 3 percent were highly successful. This same survey revealed that 27 percent of our population made no effort to plan for the future, 60 percent gave some thought to the future, 10 percent had a good idea where they were headed, and only 3 percent had actually written down goals.[2] In other words, there was a direct positive correlation between monetary success and planning for the future. The most highly effective people in the survey were those who actually wrote down goals, and this dynamic holds true in other areas of life as well.

Goals move us. In business, sports, politics, and relationship with God, goals make the difference between reaching forward with purpose, or spinning around in meaningless circles. Most people have more difficulty setting goals than they do accomplishing them once they are set. Actress Lily Tomlin once said, "I always wanted to be somebody, but I should have been more specific."

Get specific and write out some goals for yourself. Set goals in every area of your life. Set personal development goals (like exercising three times a week, learning a new language, or joining a softball league), spiritual goals, relational goals, financial goals, and career goals. The following tips will help you set and keep your goals:

1. For starters, ask yourself, "With what areas in my life am I dissatisfied?" Or "What do I really want in life?" Turn the answers into goals and write them in a journal or list them on your computer. Remember, *goals need to be specific, measurable, and attainable.*

2. Write down objectives that will help you reach those goals—these are known as subgoals.

3. Write down a new mission statement or belief that will help you reach your goals in these areas.

4. Decide how committed you are to attaining your goals. If you desire to be in peak physical condition, write out how committed you are to making this happen. For instance, write, "I am committed to eating healthy foods and exercising three times a week for the rest of my life. If I don't eat right and work out, my emotional and physical health will suffer. I will continue to be lethargic, stressed out, and depressed if I don't follow through on this commitment. But that won't happen because I am absolutely committed to getting in shape. By eating healthy and running three times a week, I will feel more alive, energized, and passionate about everything I do. I will live a long, fulfilled life because of this commitment. I will follow through no matter what!"

5. Review your subgoals daily and major goals weekly. Every morning, read your commitment to reach those goals. If physical fitness is a goal, review your commitment to this goal every day until it's a natural part of the way you live your life. If spiritual growth is your goal,

review it daily as well. As you read your commitment over and over again, you will develop strategies to help you reach them automatically. Your workout schedule may change from three times to four times a week. You may substitute swimming, walking, or aerobics for running or a favorite sport. You may study the Bible and pray in the morning some days and in the evening on others. Your game plan may be flexible but your commitment should never change.

4. Get Giving

Most people who are depressed, detached, or desperate usually don't even consider this next big "G" of giving. Think about it—when you're feeling this way, your tendency is to focus only on your own needs and wants. In this day and age of daily affirmations ("I'm good enough, I'm smart enough, and doggone it . . .") and "go hug yourself" therapy, it seems radical, if not heretical, to tell people to focus on someone other than themselves. *The key to a life of misery and loneliness is doing this one thing: seek to please yourself.*

Giving is about meeting the needs of others on a practical level. Do you seek to meet the needs of your friends and family members? Do you ask, "What can I give to this friendship," and not just "What can I get from it?" People who are grounded, grouped, and goal-oriented are also seeking to serve and meet the needs of others.

Remember the Dr. Seuss special, "The Grinch Who Stole Christmas"? The Grinch was a green, slimy character who looked like an emaciated lizard. He was born with a heart three times smaller than normal people, so he was full of anger, jealousy, and envy. But even after he stole Christmas from the Whos in Whoville, he continued to notice their joy and happiness. They kept their contentment because they gave to one another. This so touched the calloused old Grinch that he turned around and started giving Christmas back to the Whos. When he did this, his heart grew three times in size.[3]

Do you want your heart to shrink or to grow? Get outside of yourself, and start giving to others around you. You will be amazed how your own life will be enriched in the process. Speaking of growing, that brings us to the fifth and final "G" of getting a life.

5. Get Growing

In all aspects of life, things are either stagnant or growing. If you are not growing, expanding, or improving your life, you are stagnant. Almost everyone wants to be fully alive and passionate about life. But some people are little more than walking corpses, because they have *stopped* growing. Growing requires the willingness to learn, improve, explore, discover, and reach out to "boldly go where you haven't gone before."

How do you grow? It's simple. Ask yourself, "What do I have a passion for?" or "What would I want to do if I had all the money in the world and knew I wouldn't fail?" Here's a list of ways you can get growing. For more, check out Dr. Harold Ivan Smith's booklet, *51 Good Things to Do While You're Waiting for the Right One to Come Along.*

1. Learn a new language.

2. Learn to play a musical instrument.

3. Pick up rock climbing or skydiving (for the brave at heart).

4. Take dancing lessons.

5. Learn to paint, draw, or write poetry.

6. Start hunting or fishing.

7. Improve your public speaking skills.

8. Play your favorite sport or pick up a new one.

9. Continue your education.

10. Pick up sailing, skiing, or scuba diving.

11. Learn about another country and culture and then travel to this foreign land.

"Wow. This sounds risky. What if I fail?" So what? Even failure is a learning, growing experience. *Success comes from good judgment, good judgment comes from experience, and experience comes from making mistakes.* Don't worry if you aren't Kenny G, Norman Rockwell, or Steffi Graf after a month of lessons.

The key to growing is risk. Leo Buscaglia once said, "The person who risks nothing, does nothing, has nothing, and is nothing. To laugh is to risk being a fool. To weep is to appear sentimental. To reach out to others is to risk getting involved. To love is to risk not being loved in return. The person who risks nothing may avoid suffering and sorrow but he simply cannot know, feel, change, grow, live, or love."[4]

Take a risk and throw yourself into life. Seize the day. Dare to lead an extraordinary life. Start something new or rekindle an old passion, but whatever you do, never stop growing.

CONSEQUENCES OF BREAKING THIS COMMANDMENT

- You will be bored, depressed, lonely, self-centered, worried, and hopeless. And it just keeps getting worse because the longer you live the un-life, the more ill you become. Sounds pretty bad, doesn't it?

- Just in case you haven't gotten the picture, let us sum up the consequences with one final question: Would you respond to a singles classified ad in the newspaper or on the Internet that read: *SWM, overweight couch potato, unhappy, lonely, self-obsessed, withdrawn ISO [in search of] SWF, good-looking, athletic, strong Christian, outdoorsy, and a real passion for life.* Of course not! That's why you must follow this commandment. If you choose not to obey, then just expect to continue repelling the opposite sex and being unhappy.

BENEFITS OF KEEPING THIS COMMANDMENT

- When you have a life of your own, you are attractive to others. That's the first benefit of getting a life. People who exude confidence, stability, and a passion for living inevitably draw others to themselves like a magnet. This is simply a natural by-product of this first law.

- Once you get into a relationship you will greatly increase the odds of it being healthy and rewarding. Your capacity for intimacy will be enhanced, and your ability to handle the challenges that come with relationships will be strengthened. Because you have a life, you will be interesting to your partner, having something to offer that may enlighten and inform others.

- You will not put undue pressure and unreasonable expectations on your partner to meet your emotional needs and complete you. This frees you both up to be yourselves and to recognize each other as separate people.

- Ultimately, you will be content, happy, and have an inner peace. This joy will spring from you because you are passionate about life. You know who you are, you have a support system, you have direction, and you are seeking to serve others.

HeLp for you who have broken this commandment

- Relax. A mistake or two isn't the end of the world, but an opportunity for change. Let this motivate you to find a real existence. Let the symptoms of the un-life serve as a catalyst for change.

- Review the five Gs of getting a life, and take action today. Don't overanalyze the situation and paralyze yourself. Begin to take deliberate, intentional steps to pursue a life. Peace, happiness, purpose, and a passion for living will follow those who follow this commandment. You can do it. So get grounded, get grouped, get goal-oriented, get giving, and get growing. You'll be glad you did!

Commandment Two

THOU SHALT USE YOUR BRAIN

Michelle and Russell were infatuated. They couldn't get enough of each other. They had found their respective soul mates, the fulfillment of their wildest fantasies. At any given moment, they could be found joined at the hip and locked at the lip. They were in love. *But everyone else knew better.* Friends and family all insisted that these two didn't belong together. Michelle and Russell had nothing in common, they had only known each other for one month, and at this point, it was too early for a commitment to each other.

Sound familiar? Have you ever found yourself saying, "Why does she stay with that clown?" Or how about, "I thought he was smarter than that!" Most of us have experienced the frustration of watching someone we care about get involved in a relationship that just doesn't make sense. Worse yet, maybe you have found yourself in the midst of a relationship driven by nothing but raw emotion, only to find later that the relationship was doomed from the start. How do you account for

19

this bizarre activity? What is responsible for such behavior? *The culprit is romantic love.*

In this chapter we will help you distinguish between *romantic love* and *real love*. We will also tell you about three major forces of romantic love, and how some of the people who've come to us for counseling have been sucked into the Romance Vortex. Then, we will demonstrate how to avoid the pitfalls of Hollywoodized "true romance" by using your brain. *The key is using your head in matters of the heart.* Remember, your brain is located above the neck, not in the chest cavity or below your belt.

THE GRAND ILLUSION

Ah, the ecstasy of romantic love. Nothing beats that magical experience of locking eyes with the person of your dreams across a crowded room, falling head-over-heels in love, and spending the rest of your life in marital bliss. If you're not familiar by now with how this thing works, we suggest that you indulge yourself in several romantic novels. Likewise, in cutesy television sitcoms and weepy Hollywood movies the prince falls in love with the princess, they get married, and everyone lives happily ever after. It all sounds great.

There's only one small problem—this is an illusion. This doesn't happen in real life. Never has. Never will. What we are saying is that *romantic love has little to do with real love.*

Let's face it, as a society we are confused about love. We are constantly inundated with messages about love from Motown, Madison Avenue, and other media to the extent that our understanding of true love has been severely distorted. We are easily fooled into thinking that love is just a feeling. As one person put it, "It's feeling that feeling that we have never felt with anyone else." Although deep down we all want to believe the fairy tale version of love, sooner or later we must face the truth. Real love doesn't just "happen" to you. Love is not simply a feeling, it is much more.

What is real love? This is one of the great questions of life, and for centuries philosophers and theologians have tried myriad ways to define love. However, from our perspective, some of the definitions in ancient times far surpassed some of the recent silliness depicted in pop culture. The Greek culture was one step ahead of us when it came to defining love. They understood the complexity of love and that they needed vocabulary to grapple with the complexity. The Greeks were not content to talk of love in such general, vague terms as we use today. For example, they made clear distinctions between *eros* (romantic love) and *agape* (real or mature love).

According to the Greeks, *eros* is the passionate form of love. It includes all the elements of that initial attraction and romantic phase of a relationship: obsession, mystery, allure, excitement, passion. Primarily, emotion animates *eros*, rendering it quite unstable. On the other hand, *agape* is a kind of love demonstrated by two people who deeply care about each other and who are mostly concerned about the welfare of the other. *Agape* concerns a mature and stable kind of love—solid, enduring, and providing a sense of security.

Romantic love and real love are two separate and distinct conditions. Real love is a decision to seek the good of another, whatever the cost. *Agape* includes nurture, support, encouragement, acceptance, and companionship. When it comes to crafting a lasting relationship, particularly a marriage, real love far outstrips the fleeting passions of romance. *Eros* is ill-designed to bear the weight of life's stresses. We need to reject the folly of basing a marriage on such passion. Taking the time to allow *agape* to flourish, couples can build on a solid foundation of commitment, acceptance, and nurture.

VALUE IN ROMANCE?

Is there any value in romance? Absolutely! We are not down on romance and passionate love. Romance is a normal, natural part of most healthy relationships. In fact, I (Sam) will be the first to admit of making a "fool" of myself while falling in love with my wife. I know what it's like to experience the ecstasy of puppy love—to feel as though my world revolves around another person. I remember the intense physical and emotional drive to want to spend every waking moment with her. I enjoyed every minute of the romantic phase in that first six to nine months of our relationship. But that's just the point: *the romantic love was a phase, and we did not allow it to dominate the relationship. Eventually we moved on to a deeper kind of love—a mature form of love, a real love.* Real love can only begin to grow or flourish when the infatuation diminishes. And it is only this kind of love that can sustain a marriage relationship in the long run. Does this mean that romance is no longer a part of our marriage? Of course not! It just means that the romance and passion is an aspect that enhances what we have rather than functions as the foundation for our relationship. We all cherish the excitement and exhilaration that comes with getting caught up in romantic love. Perhaps without this experience men and women might never end up with each other.

However, the time has come to stop giving romantic love so much credit. *Eros* cannot measure compatibility. Romantic love tells you nothing about one's character, and it is extremely unreliable as a method for determining the viability or health of a relationship. Unbelievable as it may seem, when it comes to successful dating or marriage, romantic love doesn't necessarily mean squat!

So what place does it have in the dating experience? We believe that romance must be recognized for what it is: an introduction to someone who could be a potential mate. We like to think of it as a temporary glue that gives us time to evaluate the person we are with, to consider the more important issues of character and compatibility. Unfortunately, most people do not take advantage of this valuable opportunity, and they merrily zoom along the waves of passion all the way into serious mistakes. Couples must make a commitment up front to balance romance with common sense, reason, judgment, and discernment. You must use your head in matters of the heart. In fact, *when it comes to decisions about relationships, you should choose the head over the heart every time!*

THREE DRIVES OF ROMANTIC LOVE

We believe that romantic love consists of three very powerful drives that can interfere with our ability to use the brain: *emotions, hormones,* and *spiritual leadings.* Any of these drives by themselves or in combination can cause you to become disoriented, delusional, and even drop one hundred IQ points in a matter of seconds. What happens when you allow these drives to dictate your relationships? We will look at the following real-life love stories, and the results of disobeying the commandment to use your brain. As you will see, the consequences can be tragic and far-reaching.

1. Emotion-Driven Dating

Carl met Elaine one day by "divine fate" at a New Year's Eve party. They immediately fell head over heels in love, and became consumed with each other day and night. She felt that he was the missing piece to her life because he made her feel so complete. Likewise, he felt she was the one because she made him feel so alive. Gazing into each other's eyes, they promised themselves to each other because no one had ever made them feel THAT way, a feeling that could only be described as out of this world. Three months later they danced blissfully down the aisle of their local wedding chapel to take the vows of man and wife.

Here it gets really scary. Soon after their fast-track engagement, someone asked Elaine the following questions: "Do you know anything about his family?" "Do you even know his middle name?" Elaine chirped back, "No, but it doesn't matter because we're in love." Elaine didn't know or care to know. She was content to trust her emotions on this one. The friend tried to reason with her, but Elaine wouldn't listen. A year later Carl and Elaine became a part of the 200,000 people annually who divorce before their two-year anniversary! If only they had slowed down long enough to discover each other's family history! Sadly, they bought into the lie that romantic feelings equal love, and that those feelings last forever. Relationships built on emotionalism can be deadly.

2. Hormone-Driven Dating

Nothing interferes with logic and common sense more than the sex drive. For years we have referred to this as the Brain Relocation Phenomenon, which occurs when you are passionate about someone and you start to get intimate. Here's how it works: once the hormones kick in, the brain dislodges from the skull and slowly moves down the body, through the neck, shoulders, chest, stomach, and, finally, below the waist. This process takes ten to twenty minutes for women and about three seconds for men. But once it happens, it's too late! You are thinking and reasoning with your hormones instead of your brain.

Marshall called the radio show one night confessing his numerous premarital sexual encounters. One such encounter was with Sharon, with whom he had fallen in love. They had had a "great sexual relationship" and had recently married, but once they were married she shut down sexually. Sharon lost the much ballyhooed "romantic passion." He felt cheated and concluded that she had used sex to lure him into marriage. Needless to say, without the passion and raw sex, the basis for their relationship was now destroyed. You can't build a marriage on hormones and emotion; you must use your brain.

Another typical scenario is embodied in the case of Sarah and Chris. They had been dating for three months when Chris decided he couldn't control his sex drive. Chris went to the Bible searching for answers. Lo and behold, it didn't take him long to find "It's better to marry than to burn with lust" (1 Cor. 7:9). Thus, they tied the knot with no real basis for marriage other than the "holy" satisfaction of their sexual urges. Five miserable years and two children later, they decided to divorce because they simply didn't use their brains when they were dating. Now, two children will grow up in a single-parent household, and four people will experience the repercussions of this selfish, brainless act.

3. Spirit-Driven Dating

There is nothing quite as dangerous as deeply "religious" men or women who spiritualize their dating. We call this "spirit-driven dating." Countless people are listening to "voices on high" instead of listening to common sense. Actually, this is not being spiritual at all because true spirituality is healthy. "Spirit-driven dating" is really hyperspiritual or pseudospiritual. The following story says it all.

When Justin and Lauren started dating, everyone wondered how this guy could have landed this incredibly righteous woman. We soon learned that Justin had used the "God told me to marry you" line to get her. Justin, a radically religious man, spotted Lauren at a singles Bible study. In a "spirit inspired" moment, Justin approached Lauren, and told her that God had revealed to him that they were to get married. Lauren responded with shock and excitement. She took Justin up on his offer to pray and fast for the next week.

Six months later, against the wishes of family and friends, she married Justin. From day one they were at each other's throats, fighting and bickering about everything. They had their relationship with God in common, but were incompatible in just about every other area. Finally, after years of marriage counseling, Justin had an affair, and their "spirit-led" romance ended in a bitter divorce.

If you depend solely on your spiritual leadings, and fail to use your brain, you may easily end up in a similar situation. There are so many wedding invitations that read, "Led by the Spirit of God, Annie and Bill invite you to attend . . ." but *should* read, "Having spiritualized their emotions and sexual urges, Annie and Bill invite you to attend . . ." Without question, this is one of the most common misuses of spirituality. If God is leading one of you, then He will be leading both of you. Don't let someone else interpret God's leadings for you.

Does that mean we are opposed to spirituality in dating and making important decisions? No way! In fact, we vigorously affirm couples seeking God for guidance about getting married. The difference lies in true, healthy spiritual life versus pseudospiritual manipulation. God gave us our minds for a reason, and using common sense is indispensable when making godly decisions.

Do you see what happens to men and women when they allow themselves to be guided by emotions, sexual passion, or heavenly voices? Hearts broken, dreams dashed, children stuck in the middle. This does not have to be your life story. You can make a commitment now to use your brain through the dating process.

A Brain Is a Terrible Thing to Waste

We have identified five steps you can take to help promote maximum brain usage:

1. **B**alance the head and the heart.
2. **R**efrain from physical intimacy.
3. **A**nalyze your past relationships.
4. **I**nclude others in the process.
5. **N**ever neglect opportunities to evaluate along the way.

If you can make a commitment to implement these five steps, you will be well on your way to using your brain, not just your emotions, hormones, and spirituality.

1. Balance the Head and the Heart

We are not antiromance, antipassion, or antiprayer. You may be tired of that disclaimer by now, but we do not want to be misunderstood. The simple truth is, somewhere in the dating process you've got to push those big three aside and use your head. I (Ben) remember a particular dating relationship when

I literally sat down one evening, pulled out a sheet of paper, and began to list all the pros and cons of the relationship. Then, I listed how we benefited each other through our relationship and how we hurt each other through our relationship. I knew that on an emotional and physical level we had the right stuff—that intangible chemistry—but still, I needed to scrutinize the big picture. Sure, I could have let myself get caught up in the romance, but I had made a conscious decision beforehand that I wouldn't be led by my feelings this time. Just as eating a balanced diet, and living a balanced life will have a positive effect on everything you do, so will balancing the heart and the head when you are dating.

2. Refrain from Physical Intimacy

If you have been sexually active in the past, this may sound crazy and might be difficult for you to do at first, but in the long run you'll be extremely glad you did. We believe there is a direct negative correlation between the level or intensity of physical contact and the ability to use your brain. How do you refrain from getting too physical? Start off slowly. The idea is not to set some legalistic law or express some magical formula, but rather the goal is to do the best for the dating relationship. After years of hearing hundreds and hundreds of success and failure stories, we strongly urge these firm lines.

Don't hold hands, kiss, or hug on the first date—or even the second, third, or fourth. Really? *Really.* The longer you can refrain from physical contact, the more special it will be when it actually happens. Furthermore, this will allow you to build a solid friendship in the early stages of the relationship. Once you start getting physically affectionate, and especially once you get sexual, the friendship side of your relationship suffers and sometimes falls apart. The affectionate and sexual aspects begin to dominate, and you no longer bother to work on building the emotional intimacy necessary for a lasting relationship.

Bart and Jennifer are both committed Christians, but when they met and began to date, they experienced the typical Brain Relocation Phenomenon. Rather than waiting for a while, Bart and Jennifer plunged ahead on the first date, kissing like mad. By the end of their first month they were far down the road in the physical area, dealing with a hurried cycle of passion, repentance, and passion again. Although they got engaged, ultimately the stresses of the engagement did what the dating period did not: reveal how incompatible they were when their brains returned to their normal spots. A bitter breakup ensued.

3. Analyze Your Past Relationships

Nothing will help you learn more about your relational strengths, growth areas, and particularly the unhealthy patterns that seem to recur more than taking an inventory of your past relationships. During football season, after every game, high school, college, and professional football players huddle around projectors to watch play-by-play game film. Coaches start and stop the film over and over again, in order to critique the players' blocks, tackles, runs, and passes. They go through this often boring and painstaking process to highlight what works well, so players can build on their successes. They also go through game films for a more crucial reason: to point out mistakes and the adjustments that are needed for the next game.

Think about analyzing your previous relationships as you would watch a game film. Ask yourself general questions about the relationship: How did we meet? What did we do right? What was good about that relationship? Also, ask more specific questions about your ex-partners: To what kind of people do I tend to be attracted? What are their positive and negative characteristics? What kind of communicators have they been? How do they treat me? Then, ask the tough questions: Why did we break up? Was I to blame, or did we simply drift apart? What are some of the issues that I need to work on? Did we get too physical? How did this area affect the relationship? Did I get carried away with the emotional high of being in love, and ignore warning signs that should have been addressed?

Include *all* relationships, and compare them, looking for distinct patterns. Also, for maximum benefit, be sure to write your thoughts down, then combine your answers and summarize the results. You are looking to discover insights about your dating habits so that you might avoid mistakes in your future relationships.

Too many times people fail to take time out and do the critical and *honest* evaluation that is needed. We work on a weekly basis with people who have recently experienced a breakup, and it's heartbreaking to hear their stories. But what never ceases to amaze us is that many single-again folks have difficulty taking responsibility for the problems in the relationship. It's always refreshing to hear someone take ownership and responsibility for their part in the breakup.

When you don't learn from your past, the good and the bad, you will not grow. Many people make the same relationship mistakes over and over again because they never take the time to analyze what went wrong and how they contributed to the difficulties. Ask yourself the tough questions. Dialogue with a trusted friend or counselor. Whatever you do, look in your rearview mirror and learn from your past.

4. Include Others in the Process

Robert could have saved himself years of heartache and misery if he had only listened to his family and closest friends. For two years he was involved in a relationship with a young lady that was going absolutely nowhere. They had little in common. They fought over trivial things. He was not sensitive to her needs. And, most importantly, there was no real joy and happiness when they were together, but he just kept trying to make it work. Early on, his friends told him to get out of it, but he didn't listen.

Finally, he was eating lunch with a friend one day when out of the blue the friend asked him if he was in love. Robert said, "I don't know." His friend was direct and to the point, telling him to terminate the relationship. This "counseling" session served as a catalyst to end the relationship. Years later Robert still thanks his friend for saving his life and the life of the woman he was dating.

It's essential to get feedback from a friend, mentor, or family member. When you're in a relationship it's easy to get so wrapped up in the emotions of being in love and feeling wonderful that you ignore red flags. In fact, we suggest that you appoint at least two people to be on the "lookout" while you're involved in a serious relationship. Robert hung on to a relationship that should have lasted six months, but he simply refused to listen to others' counsel. He wasted a lot of time, energy, and money because he didn't include other people in the evaluation process.

If you have a life, and you are grouped with solid, trusted friends, then it should be natural to involve them in the process. One of the most famous religious figures who has ever lived, Methodist church founder John Wesley, was involved in a small group of men in England called the Holiness Club (what a name for a club!). The group joined in a pact not to marry someone unless each member of the group agreed this was an appropriate choice. John Wesley picked a woman against their advice and ended up having a horrible marriage. After decades of conflict and strife, his wife left him. Love can do crazy things to a person, even to someone as righteous and wise as John Wesley.

Don't ignore the input of friends, family, and fellow Holiness Club cronies. Listen to them and weigh their advice. Trust me, it can save you from a heap of pain and misery. We have heard men and women moan and groan as they reflect back on their dating life. "If only I had listened to my room-mate." "If only I had listened to my family." You do not have to live in the "If onlys" of Regret World. Include others in the process of your dating life, and you won't regret the decisions you make.

5. Never Neglect Opportunities to Evaluate

One of the most neglected parts of a relationship is evaluation. Once you include others in the process of analysis, you'll have time to think about their words of caution or affirmation and compare them to what you believe is true. Because many people allow their hormones, emotions, or "mystic intuitions" to be their guides, they rarely take time out to sit down in a sober moment and simply think about what's going on. Granted, you may feel it will spoil the thrill of being in love if you start to analyze too much, and that's partly true. You don't want to develop "analysis paralysis," but you still need to take time to evaluate. Eventually, we all get over the infatuation phase of the relationship. You know this phase—you are smiling ear to ear, but you are totally blind to your partner's shortcomings. Once you move on past this period, which usually can last anywhere from three to nine months, depending on how long your denial capabilities are functioning, ask yourself these pertinent questions:

- Do I enjoy this person as a friend?

- Is there mutual giving and sharing?

- Is there any aspect of his or her personality that I can't tolerate?

- Could I enjoy spending time with this person if we abstained from physical contact?

- Do I feel encouraged, affirmed, and challenged by this person?

- In what ways do we benefit each other?

- In what ways do we hurt each other?

- Does he or she have a bad temper or an overly large chain saw collection? (Refer to Chapter 9, "Thou Shalt Not Ignore Warning Signs.")

Use these questions and others along the way to give yourself a relationship inspection. Just as you might take your automobile in for a routine maintenance inspection, do the same for your relationship. It may be a pain to do, but, boy, is it even more painful and expensive if you don't.

Do you see the imperative of using your brain? Go with the feelings flow, and pain awaits you. Use your brain, and move into the more mature kind of love, and you will build a foundation that can undergird a dynamic marriage for life. Appreciate the passion of romantic love for what it is, but then press on toward maturity and engage your brain. After all, choosing your mate is one of the most significant decisions of your entire life.

CONSEQUENCES OF BREAKING THIS COMMANDMENT

- You will feel disillusioned and cheated when you wake up one day, and discover major character flaws in your partner.

- You will feel let down by God because He "led" you into this relationship.

- You will feel embarrassed, ashamed, and foolish because you didn't see what was going on in the beginning.

- You will have wasted time, energy, emotion, and money on someone you should have seen right through on the first date.

BENEFITS OF KEEPING THIS COMMANDMENT

- You will be capable of wise love choices as your relationship matures.

- You will more readily be able to discern dangerous dating partners and loser relationships.

- You will avoid repeating mistakes you have made in previous relationships.

- You will be able to distinguish essential character qualities from less important physical and personality traits.

HELP FOR YOU WHO HAVE BROKEN THIS COMMANDMENT

- Admit that you are an emotional, hormonal, and spiritual junkie. (Come on, admit it. We've all been there.)

- Now make that commitment to use your head in matters of the heart.

- Determine to apply the BRAIN acrostic to balance the head and the heart, refrain from physical intimacy in the early stages of the relationship, analyze your past relationships, include others in the process, and never neglect opportunities to evaluate along the way.

тноυ sнаlт
ве eouаlly
уокеd

In the movie *Grease*, Danny Zuko (John Travolta), a rebellious kid from the other side of the tracks, falls in love with Sandy (Olivia Newton John), a beautiful blue-eyed blonde with a squeaky clean image. The couple has virtually nothing in common. He's from the poor side of town, and she's from the upper end. He's a leather-jacket-wearing gang member who dates loose women, and she's a preppy cheerleader who dates the quarterback of the football team. He's a street-smart punk, and she's Miss Goody Two Shoes. The only thing Danny and Sandy have in common is their sizzling hot attraction to one another. Essentially, they fall in love and make a few compromises in each other's direction. She puts on a black leather jacket, and he joins the track team. They reunite at the end-of-school carnival, and the entire cast breaks out dancing, singing, and generally having a good ol' time while the unlikely duo drive off arm in arm into the sunset.

The "opposites attract" relationship works great on the big

screen, but in reality it's extremely difficult to pull off. Tragically, many people actually seek out an "opposites attract" kind of pairing under the illusion that this is a good way to form an enduring bond! And many who get caught in this lie often suffer painful consequences. While it is true that opposites do attract sometimes, this attraction usually doesn't hold up to the difficulties of real life and commitment. The truth is that the most healthy relationships and marriages are ones in which there are a lot of similarities between partners. That is to say, the best marriages are relationships where the similarities far outweigh the differences.

In his book *Are We Compatible?*, C. E. Rollins indicates that the most healthy marriages are those in which there is "a strong foundation of similarities in background, temperament, goals, dreams, values, and the way in which individuals managed and ordered their physical and mental lives."[1] Rollins goes on to cite a recent Gallup poll indicating some 47 percent of marriages now end with "mutual incompatibility" as the reason for the dissolution of the relationship. In other words, a lack of similarities between partners is one of the strongest factors contributing to divorce.

In counseling and working with a multitude of couples, we have discovered that there are certain types of relationships that are doomed from the start. We call these Unequally Yoked Relationships (UYRs). This chapter will expose five of the most common UYRs and then show you what to look for in order to establish an Equally Yoked Relationship (EYR).

UNEQUALLY YOKED RELATIONSHIPS

In the Bible, there is a passage that exhorts Christians not to be yoked with non-Christians. A yoke was a strong wooden bar that was placed around the necks of oxen that was then connected to a plow. The trick was to yoke together two oxen of equal strength so they could move forward to plow a field in a straight line. Unequally yoked oxen would simply move around in circles because they were incompatible. The Bible uses this metaphor to warn of the dangers of believers being "yoked" together with unbelievers—two people who are ultimately headed in opposite directions. In a similar fashion, we aim to warn you of the dangers of dating someone with vast differences. The following is a summary of the five most prevalent (and dangerous) unequally yoked relationships.

1. The Missionary Relationship

Cindy is a paralegal by day and a missionary by night. Only her mission field is not the deep, dark jungles of Africa but rather the dark nightclubs situated throughout her city. Dissatisfied with the "boring drips" and "slim pickin's" from her church singles' group, she ventures out into the target-rich environment of the big-city bar scene. Cindy is a missionary dater because she has given up on the Christians around her and seeks to find The One from outside the faith. Her faulty assumption is that all the good Christian guys are taken, and therefore she must seek out raw potential at the local singles hot spot or some other social setting in hopes of eventually converting him to the faith. We consider Cindy an "active" missionary dater because she will date anyone who meets her superficial qualifications (rich, good-looking, etc.) regardless of his spiritual or religious beliefs.

While Cindy represents the "active" missionary dater, there is also the "passive" missionary dater. This person is one who is already involved in a dating relationship or has a tendency to drift into a relationship where there is absolutely no spiritual compatibility. Rather than break off the relationship, she hangs on by rationalizing the need to stay in it in order to bring the other person to the faith. The focus then shifts toward getting this person to jump through religious hoops and buy in to the belief system. The ultimate objective, of course, is to get him to "pray the prayer." Women are especially vulnerable to this kind of relationship because men will do anything (yes, anything!) to impress a woman. If a guy needs to walk an aisle, get baptized, speak in tongues, bark, laugh, or even lick the lint out of Buddha's belly button, he'll do it just to keep the girl. Many of you are thinking, "Are all guys that conniving and deceptive?" The answer is *yes*.

Missionary relationships come in all shapes and sizes. However, *the common denominator is the need to justify the relationship on evangelistic grounds*. The "logic" behind this approach disturbs us. For starters, how ludicrous to think that you can establish a healthy bond with someone on the basis of a hidden agenda! Does it strike you as slightly dishonest and unfair to deceive another person like this? Unsurprisingly, after hanging on to these dead-end relationships, it's even more difficult to break it off in the end. The bottom line is that when there is spiritual or religious incompatibility, get out. It's too difficult to judge the sincerity of one's spiritual quest when the emotions of love and romance are involved. Missionary relationships simply don't work.

Doug was a leader in the church with winsome faith in Christ. In the course of his job, he met an attractive woman named Katy. She hit his list of characteristics in many ways, but she rejected Christ. Initially, Doug had no intention of dating her, but working together on projects, and their naturally outgoing personalities had them sharing deep stuff in their lives. The chemistry was there, so Doug and Katy began to date. Church members and leaders called him on it, but Doug rebuffed their questions. This was different . . . she was close . . . he wasn't really yoked . . .

Katy heard him loud and clear when he said he could not marry a non-Christian, but she liked him so much it didn't matter. She just kind of figured it would take care of itself. So did Doug. Months later as he studied the Bible one morning, Doug felt a clear conviction and knew that he was in an unequally yoked relationship. He broke the news to Katy, who was totally crushed. He was miserable in the aftermath, months down the drain. She was utterly turned off to Christianity, because the Christian she knew best had led her on for months before being obedient.

2. The Mother Teresa Relationship

This past year marked the death of one of the most respected and saintly women of all time, Mother Teresa. Her mission statement was simple: love and comfort the sick and dying in the streets of Calcutta. She was annually listed as one of the most admired women of the world. Tragically, some women have adopted this mission statement for their love lives. They attach themselves to men who are emotionally "sick and dying" and unable to give back. Against all odds, they attempt to love, comfort, and take care of their lovers in an effort to nurture them back to emotional health. This is what we call a Mother Teresa relationship: a well meaning person hangs on to a partner who is emotionally sick and needy.

The very foundation of this kind of relationship rests upon the dynamic of caretaking: one partner is the nurse, and the other is the patient. Often, the only similarity among partners is the mutual agreement to stay in this sick kind of relationship. Psychologists often refer to this as the codependent relationship, which is characterized by one partner attempting to take care of, control, or change the other partner. This behavior only enables or exacerbates the problem, and thus it is extremely rare that the "sick one" is nursed back to health. And in the unlikely circumstance that Mother Teresa is successful in this rehabilitation scheme, then she has essentially worked herself out of a job—she is no longer needed!

Jan is a classic case of someone who continually falls into the Mother Teresa relationship. Jan fell in love with a handsome young man who never showed her physical affection. After months of thinking this would change, she finally confronted David on this problem. He reluctantly revealed that he was a recovering homosexual and wasn't comfortable expressing affection at this point. Unfortunately, Jan did not consider this to be a red flag and eventually married David. After two years of marriage, David ran off with another man. Jan was shattered and disbelieving, because throughout their courtship and marriage she believed she could love him into health.

We could cite case after case of individuals who have had their lives torn apart because they sincerely believed they could heal a drug addict, alcoholic, or sex addict. After being warned of the dangers of this kind of relationship, one misguided Mother Teresa type said, "I have enough love for both of us."

If you have a tendency to attract and hang on to needy people in order to "love" them to health, then you need to ask yourself why. Why are you drawn to the sick and dying? Why do you have this unquenchable need to be needed? Why do you think you have the ability to change this person? You are called to be an equal partner in a relationship, not a shrink, surrogate parent, missionary, or nurse. Mother Teresa relationships may seem exciting and challenging at first, but, after futile attempts to rehabilitate a sick partner, they usually end in disillusionment. If this describes you, you need remedial work in the first commandment: Get a Life!

3. *The Exotic Relationship*

When two people from radically different cultural or ethnic backgrounds get together the result is the Exotic relationship. Gina, a top saleswoman for an international computer company, attended a weekend business seminar in Florida. It was there she met and fell in love with a successful Venezuelan entrepreneur named Juan. To Gina, he was an Antonio Banderas look-alike. She was enticed by his accent, cultural differences, and mysterious demeanor. Upon agreeing to see each other exclusively, they maintained a long-distance relationship for almost ten months. After numerous five-hundred-dollar phone bills, letters, E-mails, and even a couple of trips back and forth to see each other, Gina woke up one morning and realized she was making a colossal mistake. After some careful soul-searching, she came to the conclusion that she wasn't in love with Juan, but rather she was in love with the idea of dating someone from a different country. The relationship was based on the mystery and allure of being with someone completely different in so many ways.

Sure, exotic relationships are exciting and adventurous, but they're extremely impractical. Under the best of circumstances, dating and marriage are difficult and challenging. But when you throw in the exotic wild card of mixing different cultural and ethnic backgrounds, then you are simply asking for trouble. Before you invest time, energy, and money into an exotic relationship, consider the fact that the odds of this kind of relationship actually making it are Juan in a million.

4. *The Sugar Daddy Relationship*

The hallmark of the Sugar Daddy relationship is the substantial age difference between partners. If you find yourself saying, "Yes, sir" to your partner, then you may be in a Sugar Daddy relationship. If your mentor is Anna Nicole Smith, then you may be in a Sugar Daddy relationship. If your partner is still telling you stories about the "good ol' days" in the fifties, then you may be in a Sugar Daddy relationship. These types are usually attempting to compensate for unmet emotional needs, or expecting their partner to somehow fill in for Mom or Dad. Regardless of the psychological reasons behind this phenomenon, in most cases this substantial age gap represents an unequally yoked relationship. Frankly, there are just too many barriers to overcome in this kind of relationship. It takes enough work just to maintain a healthy relationship among partners from the same generation!

When we do conferences on this subject, someone will inevitably ask, "How many years' difference represents a substantial age gap?" There is no magic number, but if you pressed us we would say ten years is substantial. Of course this applies to singles under the age of forty, because somehow once we pass through various stages of life and enter middle adulthood, our level of maturity evens out (in theory). Subsequently, there is a big difference between a thirty-year-old dating a twenty-year-old and a fifty-year-old dating a forty-eight-year-old. Please don't get hung up on these numbers, as they are just general reference points. The point is, dating someone too young or old for you isn't necessarily "indecent," it's just extremely difficult to manage.

Sugar Daddy relationships provide a sense of emotional or financial security early on in the relationship, but eventually they hit several snags of incompatibility. Energy levels can be drastically different. Tastes in recreational pursuits often vary. Cultural connecting points such as movies, historical events, music, and past trends will also be different. These things may seem trivial, but they are important when you are seeking to build a bond strong enough to survive the storms of marriage.

5. *The Dennis Rodman Relationship*

Like it or not, pro basketball superstar Dennis Rodman has become a cultural icon and antihero to many aspiring youth in our country. Rodman is famous—or infamous, depending on your perspective—for dying his hair a multitude of colors (including fuchsia), kicking a cameraman, tattooing nearly every inch of his body, and frequently dressing up like a woman with dress, heels, makeup, etc. He is truly a rebel without a cause.

Perhaps you haven't dyed your hair lime green, engaged in random body piercing, or had a one-night stand with Madonna, but you still may be in a Rodman relationship. The essence of this kind of relationship is the need to date someone purely out of rebellion. Rodman relationship daters choose a partner who is exactly the opposite of everything their families would want for them. Let's say you were raised in a conservative, traditional, Christian home where there was a strong emphasis on prestige or financial security. However, if you generally find yourself with partners who are liberal, and irreligious types with no money, you are a repeat Rodman relationship dater.

Anna grew up in an upper-middle-class family who had a very reputable name in the community. The youngest child of six, she was constantly pampered, never allowed to make her own decisions or do things on her own. Not surprisingly, weeks after graduating from high school, she wound up in a Rodman relationship. She started dating a guy from a different country who had a criminal record. This infuriated her parents and bewildered her closest friends who counseled her otherwise, but she would not listen.

Relationships like Anna's are not uncommon. Most of the time, people like her are not in love with their partners, but merely angry with their parents or attempting to define themselves as a way to establish a sense of autonomy and independence. We believe there are more constructive ways to deal with anger or establish independence than taking a walk on the Rodman side. Save yourself the heartache, pain, and embarrassment by staying clear of any kind of Rodman relationship.

A whole book could be devoted to Unequally Yoked Relationships that are doomed to fail. We think you get the gist, so let's move on to the Equally Yoked Relationships because these are the relationships that work.

THE EQUALLY YOKED RELATIONSHIP

A relationship, by definition, is the connecting of persons. Therefore, to have a successful relationship with the opposite sex you must connect on many levels. This is what we call an EYR—Equally Yoked Relationship. Undoubtedly, you have been in relationships where there existed a partial connection—you connect on one or two levels, but you sense that something is missing. Sometimes we refer to this as the Heavy Metal Headbanger Relationship.

No, a Heavy Metal Headbanger Relationship doesn't mean you are dating someone in a rock band. It simply means that you are dating someone where almost everything is going right, but on some level you know you aren't connecting with your partner. Something is missing. So, you bang your head against the wall and kick yourself because you can't figure out what's wrong. Stop the headbanging and relax. More than likely, you are in a relationship where there is partial compatibility. We want to demonstrate that in order to truly connect with another person, you must connect on three general levels: *spiritual, physical,* and *social.*

1. The Spiritual Connection

If you cannot connect with your partner on a spiritual level, your relationship is headed for disaster. What you believe about God, how you pray, where you worship, which holidays you celebrate, which books you hold to be sacred, and your opinion on baptism are just a few components that make up your spiritual belief system. When you don't see eye to eye with your partner in these areas then you are compromising something that is deeply ingrained in you. Your spirituality and how that is expressed is the most intense and intimate part of you.

Recently, I (Ben) attended a concert at the House of Blues in Los Angeles. Above the stage was a huge sign that said, "All Is One." On each side of the slogan there were different religious symbols representing Judaism, Christianity, Islam, Buddhism, and Hinduism. This "All Is One" theme sounds great in a music venue, but it is extremely impractical if applied to the relational realm like so many do. Frankly, there are big differences between Muslims, Jews, Christians, and Buddhists, and even between Protestants and Catholics. Sure, there are some basic external, moral behaviors that ring true for most of the major world religions, but the essence of the religions differs. If the essence of two different religions lives strongly in two people, trying to get their hearts truly together is complex. That's an understatement. Consider that most of the wars being fought around the globe today are over religious issues. If you don't want your relationship to become a bloody battleground, then don't date or marry someone outside of your particular religious heritage.

From a Christian perspective, you should date only Christians. There is no exception. Everyone thinks, "But my relationship is different." Trust us, it is not. If you could just listen to the tales of relational carnage that we hear from married couples trying to keep it together as they vehemently oppose each other on an issue that stems from their deeply held religious convictions, you would flee such a dating relationship. On your side of the altar you simply can't know how incredibly contentious it gets on the other side.

Many Christians fall into the trap of dating a non-Christian because they never bother asking that person about his or her beliefs. Others simply assume that the person they are dating is a Christian because after all, "He told me he was a Christian." There is no doubt that only God knows who is a real Christian and who is not, but He does lay down a few guidelines to help you discern if the person you are going out with is a genuine Christian.

Personal testimony. Someone who knows Jesus Christ will be able to point to a certain time in life when he or she personally trusted in Him as Lord and Savior. A Christian makes a conscious decision to repent of sin and to trust and follow Christ. A believer feels no fear or shame acknowledging and discussing this critical life foundation.

Changed lifestyle. A Christian seeks to live according to the principles set forth in the Bible. Believers attend church and desire to hang out with other Christians. They seek to love others and bring them into a personal relationship with Christ.

Christians value sexual purity and don't take advantage of their partners. They desire to study, pray, and apply the Scriptures to their lives. They forgive others because they have received abundant forgiveness from God.

Be sure that you are dating a person with whom you can connect on a spiritual level. If you are a Christian, be certain that your partner has had a "real deal" encounter with Christ and, as a result, has a changed life. Tremendous joy and intimacy will flow within the couple who connects on the spiritual level. On the other hand, tremendous heartache and frustration will occur when two people are unable to connect and share this most intimate part of their lives.

2. The Physical Connection

Not only must you connect on the spiritual level, but you also must connect with your partner on the physical level. While this may seem obvious, we are asked with astounding frequency about the importance of this dimension. *Being sexually attracted to your partner is a prerequisite for a healthy relationship.* Having a spiritual connection is not enough. You must have that spark, that chemistry, that attraction that draws you to that person like a magnet.

George Harrison describes that kind of magical physical attraction in his song entitled "Something." In the song he sings about that intangible quality that must be present to sustain an enduring relationship. There must be that "something" in the way that person looks, moves, laughs, speaks, or smiles that compels you to want to be with him or her.

Most people overdose on the attraction thing (refer back to Commandment Two—"Thou Shalt Use Your Brain") and forget about the other crucial levels of connection, but still we meet people who hang on to others without any romantic attraction. John was such a person. He dated Brenda for over two years because they were such great pals. They went to the same church, shared the same friends, got along with each other's family, but something was missing in the physical area. He thought an attraction would grow, so he waited, prayed, and tried everything he could to muster up some kind of romantic connection, to no avail. Fortunately, John told Brenda it wasn't working out, and they broke up. We believe that John did the right thing. You see, there are no "Ten Steps to Developing Chemistry." All great relationships have some element of chemistry, and you either have it or you don't. Most likely you will never grow into it or somehow make it happen.

3. The Social Connection

Some people often ignore or neglect social compatibility, though this very area creates lots of stresses on relationships. Social compatibility primarily concerns family patterns and social relating, and we'll consider them in order.

Family matters. The old saying, "The apple doesn't fall far from the tree," usually holds true. Who you are and many of your perspectives (big and small) on life stem directly from your family upbringing. If you grew up in a home in which you received love, support, encouragement, and security from your parents, then you probably have a good foundation for building a relationship with another person. If you didn't grow up in such an environment, then you will have to work a little harder to develop such a relationship.

Not too long ago families stayed together, and people married their next-door neighbors, or at least someone from their hometown. One could find someone who shared similar family and cultural perspectives more easily. However, with today's overwhelming divorce rate, blended families, and frequent transcontinental moves, the difficulty in finding a partner with a similar family background skyrockets. Nonetheless, this remains a tremendously vital area for seeking compatibility because of the many related issues.

Listed below are some of the more important issues associated with family background:

- holiday customs
- family rules
- expectations about spousal roles
- finances
- rearing children
- in-laws
- domestic responsibilities
- work ethic
- resolving conflict
- religious beliefs and practices

Given the pervasive influence of one's family life, it remains all too important that you seek to connect on this level.

The other area of connecting at the social level deals with patterns of relating. This dimension of a relationship covers a wide variety of concerns, including:

- social skills
- level of social involvement
- how to spend free time (i.e., hobbies, interests)
- desire to be in groups/social gatherings

- gravitation toward similar types of people
- communication style
- intellectual compatibility/educational background

Kenneth called Ben's radio show to talk about his dating relationship. Kenneth had been dating Erica for almost two months, and he was starting to question their compatibility. When they first started going out, everything was wonderful. Erica was lively, smart and sassy, and her passion for Christ matched her stunning beauty. Over time, however, Erica began to let down her guard and manifested a bossy, demanding temperament. What was an asset in her challenging career proved unhelpful in relating to Kenneth. Kenneth felt ambushed, because early on he thought Erica was an amazing woman. He was looking for someone with whom to share his life, not a boss to direct his life. Wisely, Kenneth understood that social compatibility was important for the health of a lasting relationship. What does it mean to be equally yoked? Well, similarities between people make life together much simpler. Partnerships, by necessity, involve compromise, and people can reach these compromises more easily when they share common values and interests. This holds true whether you're going on a date and picking a movie or whether you're married and deciding where to rear your children. By contrast, being unequally yoked to someone with whom you have few affinities can turn even the smallest of decisions into big problems. Sure, sometimes opposites can attract, but for a stable relationship bet on similarity.

CONSEQUENCES OF BREAKING THIS COMMANDMENT

- You will be unable to bare your soul with the person you love the most.
- You will experience unnecessary pain, frustration, and confusion because you are dating someone who is nothing like you.
- You will drive yourself and your partner crazy because you are trying to change the unchangeable.

BENEFITS OF KEEPING THIS COMMANDMENT

- You will be able to experience the joy of true, deep, spiritual connection.
- You will be on the same page morally, socially, and mentally.
- You will minimize the stress and conflict that come with differences.

HELP FOR YOU WHO HAVE BROKEN THIS COMMANDMENT

- Relax. If we hadn't broken this commandment several times we couldn't have written this book.
- If you are in a UYR right now, apply the Band-Aid Rip method of breaking up (see Commandment Five), and prepare for God's best for you sometime in the future.

Commandment Four

THOU SHALT
take it sLow

Do you ever wonder why you get into a great big hurry the second you step foot in an airport? You rush to buy your tickets, only to wait in line for what seems like eternity. You then walk briskly to your gate, but you still have to sit down until the flight attendant calls your boarding order. You sprint to get in line to get on the plane, only to encounter another line of people in the tunnel gate waiting to board the plane. Once you get on the plane, you slow down a little until the plane lands and the demon of hurry jumps on you once again. You jump out of your seat, and reach over three people to get the sixty-pound luggage you should have checked out of the overhead compartment, and squeeze your way into the aisle only to wait forever until the plane's doors open so you may exit. Once in the terminal, you sprint like O. J. Simpson (the younger, less confused Simpson) to retrieve your remaining luggage in the baggage claim area. Of course, once you get to baggage claim, you have to wait another fifteen minutes until your luggage rolls around the bend. Then you make a mad dash to the rental car area, only to wait in line again. All the rushing, pushing, and running in reality rarely speeds up the travel process. But that still doesn't stop you from repeating the process every time you travel, as if you are thinking, "You know, this time, I'm going to beat the odds."

Similarly, the second some people step into a relationship, they feel the need to rush through the dating process as if they were running late to catch a plane. If you read in the morning paper that half of all flights in America would crash before reaching their destinations, would you be a little more cautious about flying? Most of us would probably never fly again, but every day people speed into unhealthy relationships and all the way to the altar, knowing that their relationship has a fifty-fifty chance of crashing and burning. They reason, "I know what the divorce stats say, but this time I'm going to beat the odds."

We've done premarital counseling with hundreds of couples, held weekly radio interviews with some of the top relationship experts in the country, and helped countless men and women try to pick up the pieces of broken marriages. As a result of this immersion into relationships, we're convinced that the number one reason couples divorce is not money, sex, or infidelity, but rather the decision to get married was made too quickly.

Over 950,000 Americans will die this year of heart disease, making it the number one killer.[1] Over 1.2 million Americans will divorce this year, and the number one reason for these relational deaths is the impulsive decision to get married.[2] In his book *Finding the Love of Your Life*, Neil Clark Warren cites an empirical study conducted by researchers at Kansas State University, which states, "Couples who had dated for more than two years scored consistently high on marital satisfaction."[3] The risk of marital failure diminishes significantly with longer dating periods. Yet, in the face of all the evidence, couples still think, "Our relationship is unlike any other, we're different, we'll beat the odds."

Why do so many think so similarly (and foolishly)? Furthermore, what is it about relationships that compels us to rush things?

If you have ever listened to my (Ben's) *Single Connection* radio program or attended one of our relationship seminars, you know the most important dating principle. Frankly, it's beyond the realm of principle, and it's really an essential commandment. What commandment do we pound into peoples' heads? *"Take it slow, get to know."* Take it slow and get to know the person you are potentially marrying before you buy the ring or practice how his last name sounds with your first name. *No one enters a marriage with the goal of getting a divorce, but still millions divorce.* Why? They didn't take the time to get to know the persons with whom they were going to spend the rest of their lives. If your parents were divorced, or perhaps you have been divorced, you do not have to go through that pain again. If you will take the time and diligently follow this commandment to take it slow, you can avoid the carnage that nails one out of two marriages. In this chapter you are going to discover three reasons why it is smart to take it slow, and how you can actually do that in your relationship.

THREE REASONS TO TAKE IT SLOW

1. You do not get to know a person in a short period of time.

2. You need time to bond.

3. You protect yourself from getting attached too quickly.

There is a direct correlation between length of courtship and marital satisfaction. Another study reveals that the longer the courtship and engagement period, the longer the marriage. With marriages crashing and burning all over the place, don't you want to do everything possible to reduce your risk of getting a divorce?

In college, I (Ben) fell in love with the woman I would eventually marry. I was extremely attracted to her, we had a lot in common, we thoroughly enjoyed each other's company, and we shared an intense spiritual connection. We each thought the other was flawless until the six-month honeymoon phase in our relationship ended. We eventually began to have some conflicts, noticing character flaws in one another and discovering radically different family backgrounds. Now, we could have easily gotten engaged in that initial honeymoon period, but our relationship probably wouldn't have survived an engagement, much less a marriage.

Fortunately, we didn't get married at that time, but we persevered through a long, two-and-a-half-year courtship before we took the vows of man and wife. The often harsh realities of marriage didn't hit us as hard because we had dealt with so much junk in our courtship.

Most couples don't take nearly enough time to really get to know the person they are about to marry.

1. You do not get to know a person in a short period of time.

When you marry someone, you want to know what that person is really like before you make that lifelong commitment to love for better or worse, richer or poorer, in sickness and in health, till death you do part.

If you think you can really get to know a person's true colors in a three-to-six-month dating period, then you are either psychic or psycho. Most singles who come into my (Ben) office after enduring a five-year prison sentence (a.k.a., a bad marriage), and then survive the even more tedious process of parole (a divorce), say, "I never really knew him until we got married. I simply didn't date him long enough to see what he was truly like."

Believe me, when it comes to fervent explanations as to why your relationship is different, I've heard it all. For example, (1) I know God has told you this is the one you are to marry, or (2) you have never felt this way about anyone else, or (3) you have stayed up all night talking, and you know everything there is to know about each other. Yada, yada, yada. Trust me, you still need to take it slow. It's impossible to really get to know someone in such a short period of time.

Have you ever met someone at work or church whom you liked a lot at first? There was just something about that person that drew you in, you enjoyed his or her company, you had a lot in common, you thought you were developing a potential life-long friend. And then ... One day you discovered some major glitches in that person's character. I've met people whom I thought were great at first; our friendship started to grow, and *then* I discovered they had warrants out for their arrest, others had severe chemical addictions, and still others were pathological liars. Fortunately, these were just potential friendships, not dating relationships. Still, the point is clear: it took a long time to get to know what was really going on. Discerning a person's character often takes time.

Too many people jump into marriages after a brief courtship, only to discover their mates are abusive, chronic debtors, or workaholics. It's pretty easy to fake it in a three- to six-month period. Almost anyone can put on a good act for a few months. Plus, if you throw in the most effective device for both covering a person's true character and also simultaneously destroying discernment—*sex*—then you have a formula for disaster.

A friend of ours was flying from Chicago to Dallas in one of those planes where the seats face each other. Seated directly across from him were two women who were talking about their divorces and how awful their ex-husbands were. After trying diligently to read his newspaper, my friend finally put down his paper and gently inquired, "Excuse me, ma'am, but do you mind if I ask you two questions?" She said, "No, go ahead." He asked, "How long did you date this guy before you married him?" She said, "Six months." My friend prodded again, "How long did you date him, before you moved in with him?" She replied, "Two months." He then looked at her straight in the eyes, smiled, and said, "I don't think the divorce was completely his fault." With that closer, he picked up his newspaper again as the woman's mouth dropped open so wide her chin hit the floor.

If you try to get rich quick by playing the stock market, 90 percent of the time you will lose. The stakes are similar in relationships. If you try to get hitched quick, most of the time you will get killed. Why? The safest way to make money is by investing it over a long period of time. The safest way to make lasting relationships is through investing time to get to know that person.

Don't risk, don't bet *the rest of your life* on three to six months of romantic love. The returns of that investment decision are horrible, and you can't declare emotional bankruptcy to escape the losses. Divorce pain lasts longer than you ever imagined.

It's simply impossible to get to know someone in depth in that short a period of time. You can't speed up the maturity of a vintage wine, and you can't speed up the maturity of a dating relationship. Take a tip from Ernest and Julio Gallo, who uttered these famous words, "We will sell no wine before it's time." Apply that to your love life and you won't be sorry.

2. You need time to go through the necessary stages of bonding.

Most guys can remember going to K-Mart and being wowed by photos of shiny red hot rods that graced the boxes of these model cars you had to assemble. In these car kits, the directions were very clear about what parts you were to glue together first. First, build the engine; then wait a day for it to dry. Next, build the chassis, and wait another day for it to dry. After that, add the wheels and then glue the parts together. Then, still more patient waiting for twenty-four hours so that the pieces can bond appropriately.

Okay, what eleven-year-old boy has the ability to delay gratification at that stage in life? So, what do most little guys do? They glue the entire model together in about three hours of hard work, stare impatiently at the creation for a few minutes, and then watch it slowly fall apart. Why? Little boys don't give the glue enough time to dry.[4]

Taking it slow allows you to let the glue dry in your relationship. It helps you go through the necessary bonding stages, one step at a time.

Most relationships can be broken down into four stages of bonding and attachment. The first stage is the *Scouting Stage*, which is when you are simply testing the waters to see if you like this person or not. The second stage is what we call the *Infatuation Stage*, in which you are madly in love with this person, and absolutely blind to his or her faults. Some also call this the *Honeymoon Phase* of a relationship, which lasts anywhere from three to nine months, depending how good both parties are at faking it.

The third phase is the *Reality Bites Stage*, which occurs when you wake up and realize this "perfect person" has some glaring chinks in the armor. The fourth stage is the *Fish or Cut Bait Stage*. This stage is the final one where you decide if you should marry this person, or let go.

3. You protect yourself from getting attached too quickly.

Another reason you should take it slow is that you guard yourself from getting emotionally attached to too many people. A verse in the Bible says "do not toss your pearls to swine" (Matt. 7:6). Many singles are gifted at tossing their pearls, and there are plenty of swine who are willing to catch them.

When you have an initial attraction to someone that is so strong you can feel your heart beating through your chest, it's difficult to chill and not to react to that powerful feeling. I know lots of single men and women who are romantic love junkies. They live for that indescribable, magical spark that happens when two people feel that instant sense of closeness. Many take that feeling and run with it. Spending eight hours together on the first date, allowing things to progress way too quickly in the physical area, seeing each other every single day, and on and on. This is a formula for short-term pleasure, long-term pain.

Of course, one day they wake up and realize they are absolutely sick of being with this person, because they smothered each other so much that the love flame was extinguished. Others have a worse fate: they never slow down long enough to catch a breath, and the next thing you know they find themselves dressed in a tuxedo or a white dress about to pledge their lives to someone they have known for a whopping four months. And they think this is intelligent.

If you take it slow early on, then you won't become a love junkie or marry someone you barely know. When you seek to take it slow, you hold off any physical affection until you are ready to enter an exclusive dating relationship. This protects you from giving your heart and body to someone you don't really know. This allows you to get out of a relationship without having invested too much emotional and spiritual energy on the wrong person.

Darrell was a twenty-nine-year old single who had a sexual history longer than *War and Peace*. He finally got fed up with scattering himself sexually with various women, and getting into relationships too quickly. So he made the wise choice to refrain from romantic intimacy until he was ready to date a person exclusively. This may sound a bit prudish or old-fashioned to you. However, if you have a truly open mind and consider the number of divorces, single-parent homes, and sexually transmitted diseases that the "new-fashioned" way of dating produces, you realize that the new way just isn't cutting it. At least, we should be able to agree that the recent perspectives are failures.

Do yourself a favor and take it slow; don't throw your pearls before swine. You'll make a lot of friends, and save your heart, soul, and body for the right one.

SEVEN SLOW-MOTION DATING STRATEGIES

Because of the natural tendency to speed at the beginning of a relationship you must have a strategy locked in place to help you keep it in low gear. Here is our list of seven strategies that must be employed.

1. Make the two-year commitment (see Hezekiah 4:35).

2. Make your first date short and casual.

3. Don't volunteer too much information up front.

4. Delay physical affection.

5. Stay connected with your friends.

6. Do not pray together.

7. Don't mention the "M" word.

1. Make the Two-Year Commitment

Nothing will help you take it slow more than deciding before you go out and get involved that, no matter how great it feels, no matter how fast your hormones are pumping, no matter how many inner voices and divine ones tell you "This is the one," you are going to invest two years of your life in getting to know this person before you commit to marriage. This does not mean you should strive to enter a long, drawn-out relationship with every person that you meet. It simply means that when you believe you have found the right person, you allow for at least two years from you first date to your wedding date.

Knowing that you are in this thing for the long haul will prevent you from giving yourself too quickly to the wrong people. Having this rock-solid commitment will give you the discipline to take it slow early on because you are in no rush. You know that speed kills on the freeways and on lovers' lane, too.

Tony and Marla were a couple who did it the right way. They fell head over heels in love, and enjoyed the ooshy-gooshy stage of their relationship as long as it would last. They were attracted to each other, they were spiritually and relationally compatible, but they knew they needed the time to let the glue dry. It would have been easy for them to get engaged during that three- to six-month honeymoon phase of their relationship, but they had the smarts to take things slow. Eventually, they got married after dating about two years. They are still married, and doing very well, because the foundation of their relationship was secure.

The two-year commitment often freaks out singles and single-again people who feel like they are going to explode if their urge to merge is not satisfied soon. However, just think of this commitment as a long-term investment that will pay handsome dividends into your emotional, spiritual, and relational bank. What is a short two years in a thirty-year marriage?

If you speed through the dating process and marry the wrong person, your life will be a living hell for a long, long time, whether you stay married or get divorced. If you invest two years in that person, and follow the commandments in this book, then your life will be heaven on earth, because you will know that person for what he or she is really like. Also, you will have the confidence you are marrying the right person.

2. Make Your First Date Short and Casual

I (Ben) made some of the most ridiculous mistakes of my life on first dates. I used to get real intense, ask deep questions, and stay up half the night trying to solve the world's problems on first dates with women I barely knew. Finally, after falling in love countless times and having others fall in love with me when I really didn't even like them, I got a clue, and started making my first dates a lot shorter and a whole lot more casual.

When you start off slow, it's a whole lot easier to continue that process. Go out to lunch with someone on a first date, or give yourself a curfew if the date is in the evening, and stick to it.

Another way to keep it slow in the beginning is to limit the number of times you see a person in a week. This will serve two purposes. First, it will force you to take it slow and easy so that you don't attempt to bond too quickly. Second, you will probably become more attractive to the person you are seeing because you will not appear to be overly dependent on a relationship to make you happy, i.e., the other person will be able to tell that you have a life.

3. Don't Volunteer Too Much Information Up Front

Too many eager daters spill their guts to a potential partner on the very first date. Don't take the, "Hi, my name is Chris, let me tell you my darkest childhood memory, and why I hate my father" approach with someone you don't even know. When you share too much too soon, it's as if you are verbally vomiting on that person.

Many singles justify their proclivity to verbally vomit on the first date by saying, "I'm sick and tired of playing games. I want to be real and transparent." Listen, there is a time to be open and vulnerable, but it's not when you are just getting to know someone. Have some dignity and self-respect. Practice patience and prudence. There is another term for people who volunteer too much information up front: drunk.

4. Delay Physical Affection

Holding hands, hugging, and kissing should be symbols of a secure relationship, not a means of *gaining* a secure relationship. The minute you bring physical affection into a dating relationship, things change, expectations increase, and communication shuts down. The art of taking it slow means you are committed to getting to know a person gradually and growing into a mature friendship.

When you bring touch into your relationship, the stakes increase, and it makes ending the relationship all the more difficult. The Icing on the Cake Theory says that affection should be the finishing touches of a secure friendship that is budding into a committed dating relationship. One of the best things my wife and I ever did when we were dating was to refrain from kissing until we had gone out for three months. That three-month period allowed us to get to know each other on a friendship level, and to build a foundation that could handle physical affection. In a day when most men expect to have sex after the third date this may sound archaic, but it's the only way to develop healthy dating patterns.

Women especially need to take a firm stand here and not cave in to a man's advances. Far too many women have had the audacity to say to me, "Well, if I don't have sex with him, he'll leave." Fine—let him leave! *If you allow a man to have his way with you, you will never, ever be respected by him.*

Ultimately, men are looking for a CAR.

C- Men are looking for a *challenge*. When you hold hands with him on the first date or let him kiss you, then you are no longer in the hunt.

A- Men are looking for someone to whom they are *attracted*. Attraction has more to do with your personality and character than how you look. Sure, guys ogle and go wild over *Cosmo* supermodels at an initial glance, but in the long haul they are looking for a best friend, not merely a pretty face.

R- Men are looking for a woman they can *respect*. When

you give in to them in the physical area, you immediately
lose their respect.

*Memorize James Dobson's immortal quote, "We crave those things
we cannot attain, we disrespect those things we cannot escape."*[5]

5. Stay Connected with Your Friends

One of the worst things you can do in the dating process is
to ditch your friends the moment you feel like you've met
someone special. Maintaining your gender-specific friendships will prevent you from getting sucked into the relational
speed zone. When some people fall in love they have a tendency to punt their friends and OD on their new romantic
interest. This kind of behavior usually hacks off their friends
and scares off the potential romance. Stay connected with your
friends. You may need them on the flip side, not to mention
the fact that you will definitely need their advice and feedback
throughout the dating process. Another reason you don't
dump your friends: you will need them if and when you get
dumped.

6. Do Not Pray Together

The "let's be prayer partners" approach sounds sweet and
spiritual on the surface, but can actually be used as a form of
manipulation. Praying is one of the most intimate experiences
you can ever have. Consider the fact that when you pray with
someone you hardly know, you are encouraging a bond that
can be more intense than even physical affection or sex. There
is a fine line between spirituality and sexuality, and people
who do not respect that line are in danger of getting burned.

Let's say you have an intense attraction to someone you
have met at church. He finally asks you out, and you gleefully

accept. After dinner and a movie, he takes you back to your apartment, and you proceed to talk a little while in his car. After a while, you get out of the car, and instead of trying to hug you or kiss you, he says, "Let's pray and thank the Lord for our day." Well, you are absolutely shocked. Not only is he *not* trying to put a move on you, he is taking the spiritual lead by initiating prayer. Here's where it gets dangerous. Once you start to pray together, you are combining two of the most powerful forces on the planet: your spiritual drive and your sex drive. It's so easy for the two to get convoluted, and for you to finish the prayer session with a divine word from God that this is The One. In fact, all that you really achieved was a spiritualization of your hormones. Take it slow with prayer. There will be plenty of time down the road to pray together. Don't mess it up before your relationship has a chance to grow.

7. Don't Mention the "M" Word

If you really want to create emotional chaos and unrealistic expectations in the early stages of a dating relationship, then just mention the "M" word. The "M" word is *marriage*. Guys, whenever you drop the "M" word into a conversation with the person you are dating, you have a window of about one month to buy the ring and ask her for her hand. Ladies, whenever you drop the "M" word into a conversation with your boyfriend, you have about one week before he backs away from the relationship, mumbling as he backpedals, "I just need some space."

Never talk about marriage in the early stages of the relationship. Once you throw out the "M" word, you can't take it back or reel it back in. It changes the entire relationship, and it puts undue pressure on the two of you. Men will sometimes manipulate women by making a passing remark like, "Maybe some day we will get married," and the women often fall for the line as if it were an inevitable truth. Women, on the other hand, sometimes scare off potential partners by talking about marriage with men before the relationship has had a chance to mature. The bottom line is, keep your mouth shut. No matter how difficult it may be; no matter how many little coincidences have occurred that prove you are destined to be united; no matter how many divine revelations you receive; in spite of the comments and hints dropped by overeager parents and well-meaning friends, resist till the end. Wait. Don't talk about marriage until the timing is right.

consequences of breaking this commandment

- You damage friendships with the people who you'll need to have around once you *do break up*.

- You risk entering into a marriage and then one day waking up to see a stranger lying beside you.

- You potentially push someone away by smothering them or appearing desperate.

- You risk being deceived by someone with impure motives.

benefits of keeping this commandment

- You'll avoid jumping into a marriage with someone you don't really know.

- You'll avoid being manipulated and controlled emotionally, physically, and spiritually.

- You'll avoid the heartache of emotionally or physically bonding with someone too early and scattering yourself.
- You'll experience more enjoyment in seeing a relationship develop gradually rather than rushing through it.

help for you who have broken this commandment

- Put on the brakes in your relationship—it's never too late to slow things down.
- Work on maintaining or re-establishing your same-sex friendships.
- Set clear physical boundaries.
- Commit to date throughout the "seasons" and take time to let it grow.

Commandment Five

tHOU sHaLt set cLeaR BOUNDaRies

"He ran over you with his motorcycle?" I exclaimed at the top of my lungs, responding to one of the most outlandish calls I have ever received on the radio. "Yes, that's right," Brooke replied with a soft voice. "But you see, that was two years ago, and now he's really changed," she continued before I unloaded on her again. "Brooke, do you hear what you are saying? This guy is a maniac who should be behind bars, and you are wondering whether or not you should go back to this loser. *The man tried to kill you! He ran over you with a motorcycle, for crying out loud!* Case closed. Next issue please."

Even though Brooke survived the attempted Harley Davidson homicide, she went groveling back to this creep and was having sex with the guy as if nothing had ever happened. To say the least, this young lady was having difficulty setting strong relational boundaries. Now, you may have never been run over by a motorcycle madman, but if you fail to set clear boundaries in your relationships, you will feel as if you have been hit by a

Mack truck. If you can relate to any of the following statements, you are struggling with big-time boundary issues:

- "I seem to have the hardest time saying no to people I'm in love with."
- "When she's in a bad mood, I get in a bad mood too. It just ruins my whole day."
- "I've noticed that my boyfriends always take advantage of me. I must be picking the wrong guys."
- "I know what's best for him, and I'm determined to change him if it's the last thing I do!"

The common denominator in all of the situations mentioned above is one of responsibility. If you take too much responsibility for your partner or fail to take enough responsibility for yourself, then you have serious boundary problems. This fifth law of relationships has to do with being able to define yourself and maintain your sense of separateness within a relationship. Setting clear boundaries helps you to know what to take responsibility for, and it helps others know how to relate to you more effectively. If you fail to take responsibility, then watch out because you are about to be run over.

In this chapter, we will explore what boundaries are, four areas in which we all must set boundaries, four myths that say drawing lines is wrong, and we will look at the role of boundaries in a breakup.

WHAT IS A RELATIONAL BOUNDARY?

Boundaries define who you are, and they reinforce the idea that you are separate and distinct from others. They describe what you think and feel, as well as what you are willing to do. They also define your preferences, what you like and dislike, what you will accept and won't accept. They inform you as to where you end and others begin. Most importantly, boundaries help you determine for what you are and are not responsible. A *healthy dating relationship* REQUIRES *good, solid, and well-defined relational boundaries.*

Suppose you own a home and, for whatever reason, you do not have clearly marked property lines. You want to put in a swimming pool (you're in deep fantasy now), and your neighbor wants to put in a tennis court. However, neither of you knows where one property ends and the other begins. To make matters worse, you have failed to communicate your plans with each other. Imagine the confusion, conflict, and possible legal issues that would ensue between you and your neighbor. You would be in a colossal mess. Dating relationships can be just as messy, if not more so, if you fail to set clear boundaries. If you have skid marks running across your heart from previous relationships, then you need to learn how to set firm relational boundaries.

HOW TO STOP PEOPLE FROM RUNNING OVER YOU

The only way to stop people from running all over you is to let your yes be yes, and your no be no. *Boundaries are about drawing lines.* Have you ever made someone so ticked off that he or she said, "Hey, that's where I draw the line. Enough is enough!" Too many daters don't know how to draw the line, when to draw the line, or where to draw the line. Here are a few areas where you must learn how to draw the line and let your yes be yes and your no be no. Follow these principles, and you will become a healthy Line Drawer, a dater who sets appropriate boundaries.

1. *Your body belongs to you.*

You must draw definite lines in the physical/sexual area, or you will get blitzed in the dating process. We cannot underestimate the importance of clearly defining limits in this area. At the risk of insulting your intelligence, let's begin with the understanding that your body belongs to you. You alone are responsible for your body. We're talking about the ability to define what your limits are before you even step out the door on a Friday night. Physical boundaries include the ability to say no when your partner wants to go beyond what you believe is appropriate. If your partner does not respect your boundaries (i.e., you find yourself saying, "What part of 'No' don't you understand?"), consider this a *blatant* violation of your boundaries. Tell your partner to back off. If he has so little respect for you that the response to your boundaries is callous disregard, get rid of him. Your relationship will get more hellish if you try to exist with that disrespect.

If you don't set your boundaries before all the heavy breathing starts, then it will be difficult to stop that person from running over you. Just look what happened to Jean Anne. When Jean Anne was in high school, she was one of the most popular girls in school. She was the head cheerleader, captain of the swim team, and a member of the National Honor Society. She also had very high moral standards and made a firm commitment to remain sexually pure until she married. She dated many guys in high school and had one steady boyfriend for over a year, but never got too physical. However, when she left home for college she met a guy named Trenton who started to test her physical boundaries. They began by kissing passionately for hours on end, and then it progressed to foreplay. He told her, "As long as we don't have intercourse, everything else is okay." After six months, they broke up, and Jean Anne felt guilty and ashamed of what she had done with Trenton.

A year later she met another guy at a fraternity party, and she began to do the same things with him that she had done with Trenton. One night things got intense as they were making out, and she let down her final boundary and had sex with him. Looking back on the event two years later, Jean Anne was in tears because she had given away something that she can never get back.

Like Jean Anne, most people don't lose their boundaries overnight. It's a gradual process of compromise and rationalization, then the next thing you know you are giving your body and soul to someone you really don't even know. In the sexual area you must make the commitment now to draw the line. Once you are in the heat of passion the Brain Relocation Phenomenon kicks in, and you begin to reason with your genitals and not your brain. God has given you a body, and whether you like your body or not is irrelevant to the issue of being a good steward of it. Respect yourself and the person you are with. We'll talk more about sex in Commandment Six, but for now take ownership of your body and remember that it belongs to you.

2. Your emotions belong to you.

Emotions are strange animals that often seem unpredictable and uncontrollable. However, you and I are still responsible for our emotions and how we express them in our relationships. It sounds silly to state that your emotions "belong to you," but you would be surprised by the number of people we talk with every week who don't know where their emotions end and their partners' begin. Some allow their partners to intrude on their lives to an absurd degree, basically controlling their lives. Others feel the need to do just that for others, stepping in and feeling responsible for their boyfriend or girlfriend. The Boundary Police will cite you for a violation either way because *your emotions belong to you.* Thankfully, we have a few fundamental keys for setting good emotional boundaries in dating relationships.

First of all, you need to be able to communicate how you feel to your partner. *The ability and willingness to identify and express what you are truly feeling is probably the single most important factor in promoting intimacy within your relationship.* Simple expressions like, "I feel afraid," "I feel sad," or "I feel lonely," are very powerful statements, and they serve to let others know you on a deeper level. Please don't try these statements out on a first date (go slow), but once you progress in the relationship you should have the freedom to express the way you feel to your partner.

Second, you need to own your feelings and be able to separate them from your partner's. If you discover that your feelings are somehow dictated by your partner's actions or emotions, then you are too emotionally connected to your partner. You are allowing another person to control your emotional state. In short, your partner's emotional atmosphere determines whether or not you are going to be in a good mood or a bad mood.

Vince was a people-pleaser who fell in love with Zoe, a young lady with a ton of emotional baggage. If Zoe was down in the dumps when Vince picked her up for a date, then he would simply adapt his emotions to accommodate her. Throughout their courtship, Vince never was able to separate his emotions from Zoe. He would often waste entire days at work, gazing into his computer screen because he wasn't able to pull Zoe out of her emotional ditch the night before.

When you find yourself saying things like, "When my girlfriend is sad, it just ruins the entire evening" or "When my boyfriend is angry and irritable, I get angry too," you are not drawing the line between yourself and your partner. No one should have that much control over your emotions. Remember . . . you own your emotions.

Certainly there are times when we all need to exhibit compassion and feel someone's pain, but what we are talking about here goes way beyond that. The failure to own your emotions turns you into an emotional chameleon. Chameleons are those tiny lizards that take on the color of whatever they are perched on. When you actually take on the negative emotion that your partner is experiencing, as though it were contagious, you are becoming an emotional chameleon. A Line Drawer is able to separate himself emotionally from another.

3. Your thoughts belong to you.

The last time we checked, the concept of thought control and mind reading was still only a subject for science fiction novels or TV psychics. No one can think your thoughts for you. No one can know your thoughts unless you choose to reveal them. You are 100 percent responsible for your thoughts. Mental boundaries are all about taking ownership of your thoughts, and not expecting others to read your mind.

If you repeat belittling thoughts to yourself such as, "No one would ever want to go out with me" or "I'm never going to find The One," then you will reap the expected consequences of those distorted thoughts: no dates! "As he thinks in his heart, so he is" (Prov. 23:7) is truer than most of us want to believe. You are the sum total of your thoughts. You are responsible for keeping your mind clean and uncluttered. It is crucial that you take charge of your thought life and reprogram your mind, if it is full of self-condemning thoughts or self-defeating prophecies.

Another aspect of owning your thoughts is not expecting others to read your mind. Marcia never clued into this throughout her seven-month relationship with Jim. She always expected Jim to know her likes and dislikes and why she was in a bad mood. Jim bailed on the relationship because he got tired of trying to play the role of an empathetic psychic. Even after the breakup, Marcia blamed Jim for their lack of communication, not realizing that she was the real problem.

This "If you really loved me you would know what I'm feeling" mentality is ludicrous. You can't expect or assume that a person can instinctively know what you are thinking or feeling at a given time. If you are ticked off or want to do a certain activity and your partner is not catching the clues, then just say it. Don't play charades if he doesn't get it. Learning how to take control of your thoughts on one hand, and how to express them to your partner on the other will make your relationships run smoothly.

4. Your actions belong to you.

One of the most foolish things we attempt in relationships is try to change the other person. Do you ever catch yourself trying to mold and shape your partner as if he or she was a piece of clay? You must be responsible for *your* behavior, and let others be responsible for theirs.

A friend of mine once said, "You can't teach a pig how to sing. All you will do is frustrate yourself and irritate the pig." Apply that proverb to your dating relationships without hesitation. Is it really *your* job to try to change, mold, heal, fix, or reform the person you are dating? Heck no! If you don't like what you see, then move on down the line, because it is sinful and wrong to oppress other people by trying to control them. Don't hack off the pig and bang your head against the wall.

WHERE THE RUBBER MEETS THE ROAD

Drawing lines and setting firm boundaries are as simple as 1–2–3 when you are reading a book or taking a break from relationships, but somehow things go haywire when you fall in love again. While our advice is hard won over time, we recognize that it will take time and repeated failures to become a healthy Line Drawer. Boundaries for people who struggle with saying *no* don't come easily . . . but they do come!

Leslie was a twenty-eight-year-old sales manager for a large computer company. She was assertive and responsible on the job and had established herself in the industry as a quite capable worker. Her life seemed wonderful until she began a serious relationship with Calvin. Even though she was madly in love with him, she found herself constantly overextended, frustrated, and depressed, which puzzled her to no end. Calvin was polite, sensitive to her needs, and mature compared to the guys she had dated in the past. He was her dream boat, but she suspected her distress was somehow linked to this new relationship. Leslie shared her troubles with a close friend, and at the suggestion of her friend, finally agreed to get help.

Through counseling, I (Sam) discovered that she had sacrificed many things that were important to her in order to please Calvin. She had set aside her commitment to her own church to join him at his favorite place of worship. She stopped exercising at the gym because she wanted to spend her free time getting to know Calvin. She confessed that even though he wasn't demanding, they usually did what he wanted to do. She reasoned that she did not really care, as long as they were together. During most of their arguments, she gave in to keep the peace. She was even unwilling to discuss issues that she felt strongly about.

In short, Leslie had temporarily set aside her boundaries in the name of love and romance. She had lost herself while in the relationship and, as a result, was experiencing a lot of emotional pain. She was no longer drawing the line. She failed to take ownership of her emotions, thoughts, and actions and was paying a price. This is what happens when you allow romantic love to engulf you completely and wash away the lines you had drawn to keep the relationship in balance. You simply get run over.

BOUNDARIES AFTER THE BREAKUP

Even people who are healthy Line Drawers can get flagged by the Boundary Police in the wake of a breakup. Unless the breakup is one of those scorched earth wars, one side or the other often eventually feels the temptation to seek closeness with the ex. The one who initiates the renewed contact deserves most of our whipping, but the one who allows the contact merits a few lashes as well. We're not saying it's easy to draw hard and fast lines between you and your former boyfriend or girlfriend. However, it is critical that you set up boundaries after the breakup for the good of both people.

This is the Band-Aid Rip method at work. Post-relationship singles ignore the Band-Aid Rip method at their peril. Just think back to when you've had a Band-Aid on your skin covering some wound. When it comes time to remove the thing, you have two choices (but really only one if you want to mini-mize the pain!). You can peel back a little corner, and pull a little, grimace, pull a little more, grimace some more, pull some more, and slowly, excruciatingly, remove the Band-Aid. Or you can rip the thing right off in one fell swoop, quickly, and with only one grimace. The pain is still there, intensely, but it's gone in a moment, and you're soon back to normal.

It's the same in a breakup. You can have a climactic, deci-sive breakup talk, hurt like crazy, and move on. Only when you move on will both sides be able to begin the healing process. But if you don't rip, and instead slowly peel and gri-mace, you will cause pain over a long time and keep putting off the healing process indefinitely. Pain brings clarity and clarity brings closure. Both the one who did the breakup and the one who got left need to put up impregnable boundaries with each other. Outside of unavoidable functions at work or church, you should not interact with each other at all. *Zero interaction!* It sounds harsh, but it's really the best way to begin healing, which is not harsh at all. The lasting pain comes from foolishly thinking you can still be friends, or hoping the ditcher will change his or her mind, or wickedly scamming some "I need a quick fix" intimacy off the ditched. Ultimately, both sides need to set up firm boundaries after the breakup for the benefit of both sides.

FOUR LIES PEOPLE BELIEVE ABOUT BOUNDARIES

The whole concept of relational boundaries is sometimes dif-ficult to understand and apply. As a matter of fact, many of us believe certain things about boundaries that are simply not true. Here is a list of the top four lies people believe about boundaries.

Lie #1: Boundaries Are Walls

If you think setting boundaries is a way of putting up walls, we have totally miscommunicated. That is not our point at all. *Walls* keep others out; walls isolate. Why build walls? We build walls to prevent others from getting close, and if you can't be close you kill any chance at communication and intimacy. Walls are bad.

On the other hand, *drawing lines* lets others in, but with certain parameters for your safety. This is a way of enhancing communication or intimacy because it helps others know how to relate to you and move toward you in the most effective manner.

Lie #2: Boundaries Are Selfish

Granted, we will all struggle with selfishness until we have both feet in the grave. Selfishness means being "all about me." Selfishness entails excessive concern with yourself and your own needs without regard for others. Consider this statement from Scripture: "Do nothing out of selfish ambition or vain conceit, but in humility consider others better than yourselves. . . look not only to your own interests, but also to the interests of others"(Phil. 2:3–4)

Conversely, setting boundaries is *not* selfish. Setting boundaries merely forces you to take responsibility for yourself and your own needs, but at no point does this require you to ignore others' needs.

Here's the shocker: people who have a good sense of their own boundaries and how to set them are *more in touch* with the boundaries of others. That's right! You can serve better when your own sense of well-being is grounded in God and in appropriate boundaries. Secure, you are free to turn your attention to equally appropriate interaction with others. You serve them by respecting the lines they've drawn.

Lie #3: Boundaries Are Controlling and Manipulative

You don't like controlling, manipulative behavior? Then just take a try at drawing lines. Fearless line drawing *liberates* people from control and manipulation. Assert your boundaries in relationships, and you can let go of the need to control. Draw lines, and you can let others take responsibility for their own lives.

Contrary to the lie that boundaries are manipulative, boundaries respect others' choices about their own behaviors. Also, drawing lines deepens the realization that you have the choice to allow or not allow certain behaviors within a relationship. As an example, if you are on the phone with someone who constantly criticizes and abuses, and that person refuses to change this behavior, you hang up. There is nothing controlling about that. Boundaries keep others from manipulating you.

Lie #4: Boundaries Are Insensitive and Rude

If you have come away with the belief that it is okay to do whatever you want whenever you want because it's your life, consider this: Certainly, we do have an effect on others, and therefore we should always be sensitive to how our actions affect the lives of other people. But we cannot take responsibility for how others feel. You are responsible *to* others, but you are only responsible *for* yourself. There is a tremendous difference between these two.

The classic example is when one partner avoids ending a relationship because he or she is afraid of hurting someone's feelings. If you know it is time to end a relationship, the most loving and sensitive thing you can do is breakup. You are responsible to breakup in a caring, compassionate manner, but you are not responsible for your partner's emotional reactions.

And besides, the nature of a breakup is hurt feelings—it is normal to experience loss.

CONSEQUENCES OF BREAKING THIS COMMANDMENT

- You will feel used and controlled by the people you date.
- You will feel frustrated, confused, and angered because you let others dictate your emotional environment.
- You will suffer emotional and physical harm because you did not draw the line when it came to protecting your body.

BENEFITS OF KEEPING THIS COMMANDMENT

- You will build intimate relationships and still maintain a healthy sense of self.
- You will feel more secure for taking ownership of your body, emotions, and thoughts.
- You will be in control of your own schedule and how you spend your time.

HELP FOR YOU WHO HAVE BROKEN THIS COMMANDMENT

- Stop taking responsibility for others' lives.
- Practice saying "No" with people you can trust.
- Let others speak for themselves and stop speaking for others.
- Take control of your schedule and don't let your entire world revolve around the person you are dating.

Commandment Six

тноυ sнаlt save sex for Later

In the early 1960s singles were liberated to "do it," to have sex. A transformation took place in which traditional norms of behavior began to give way to a new culture of freedom and experimentation. For singles in this culture it became acceptable to have sex outside of marriage. In the '70s, during the Disco Era, living out the new uncomplicated freedoms of the '60s—doing it with whomever one wished—seemed to be nearly universal practice. It was a "feel good" era, and the old fetters of social constraint were flung off in favor of the simple feeling of pleasure.

But in the '80s, things got complicated.

People were definitely still "doing it," but a few letters like STD and HIV began to peer ominously over the scene. Suddenly, free sex had a steep price. Many dismissed the naysayers and alarm sounders as emissaries of the religious Fun Police, so they immersed themselves all the more in their "free" sexual expression. But the statistics piled up, and more and more singles picked up unexpected luggage in the form of syphilis, gonorrhea, chlamydia, herpes, and a dozen other brand-new sexually transmitted diseases. Worse still, numerous sexual adventurers were ambushed by the deadly AIDS virus.

Complicated, indeed. The runaway train of unrestrained hedonism suddenly got jolted back on track. Sex samplers discovered that the threat of AIDS had a funny way of applying the brakes in a hurry. While not everyone gave up on sexual indiscretion, pessimism made inroads into many social scenes.

Oh, but thank goodness for the '90s! Now we have a sexual savior riding into town on a white horse. Educators, politicians, and even some clergy bow down at its feet to worship this new cure-all for the country with the uncontrollable libido. Enter the Latex Messiah—the condom.

The gospel of the Latex Messiah promises to turn the complicated '80s' sexual issues around. Once again, sex is simple. The condom appears to be the only way singles can enjoy the thrills and chills of illicit sex without the nasty side effects of diseases and babies. If former U.S. Surgeon General Jocelyn Elders can be believed, telling teens and singles to wait for marriage is impossible, stupid, and maybe even criminal.

In the last three decades, we have lost the transcendent meaning of sex. Hugh Hefner, Dr. Ruth, Madonna, and Howard Stern have pushed the sexual envelope to an all-time low. No subject is more talked about, written about, studied, researched, and practiced than sex. The tragedy is that people who have devoted such a hyperattention to this sensitive subject still do not have many clues about its true nature.

Since God invented sex in the first place, one would think the church might have some answers. However, the basic party line espoused from most of its pulpits is simply "No." If you are single, God's plan for your sexual life is simple: "Wait until you get married. I know it's going to be difficult, but that's the law."

Whom should you listen to: Mainstream society, which says, "Have sex, but be careful always to wear a condom" or the church, which says, "No, wait until you get married"?

Obviously, we believe that you should save sex for later—more specifically, for marriage. But if you're like we were growing up, you need to know why. If abstinence is the right choice, the smart choice, why does it seem like everyone is having sex? Is mainstream America really that naive? Why should you wait anyway? Is there a positive reason to save sex for marriage?

In this chapter, you will discover—why so many singles are sampling the sexual waters, why you should save sex for marriage, and how to set clear sexual boundaries.

WHY SO MANY SINGLES ARE HAVING SEX

Why, apart from the fact that sex feels so good, are so many singles having sex these days when the risk is greater than it has ever been? We believe most people are doing it these days because they have bought into one of The Seven Blunders of the Sexual World:

1. All you need is a condom.

2. You've got to have it.

3. Sex equals intimacy.

4. If you are in love, it's okay.

5. You must sample the goods.

6. It's just a physical thing.

7. Everybody's doing it.

1. All You Need Is a Condom

If you want to have safe sex, which means you don't want to die of a disease or produce a baby, the Sex Gospel of the '90s says strap on the Latex Messiah and worry no more. What a colossal blunder! Here are some facts about condoms.

Condoms fail at least 10 percent of the time to prevent pregnancy. Multiple studies involving monogamous couples using a condom during every single incident of intercourse for six to twelve months have shown that the *condom failure rate is at least 10 percent, if not more.* That's for couples participating in a scientific study who had to use condoms every single time they had sex. In the real world, people tend to be more careless.[1]

In the study, 10 percent of the women became pregnant even though they used a condom every time they had sex. What is so startling about this statistic? The fact that women are only fertile for a few days of the month! During the woman's window of fertility each month, which is only about five days, the condoms are failing 10 percent of the time. What if a woman could become pregnant *every day* of the month? The minimum 10 percent condom failure rate applies to pregnancy, which couldn't even happen the other twenty-five days.

Condoms fail more *than 10 percent of the time to prevent STDs.* Do you know anyone who really would willingly place one bullet in a chamber of a revolver, spin the chamber, place the barrel in his mouth, and then pull the trigger? The very idea of being so cavalier with a life is strange and frightening.

Catch this: while the odds of getting HIV or some other STD are not as bad as 1 out of 6 (as with Russian roulette), *they are not much worse.* Based on condom failure rate for pregnancy, your sexual roulette odds with the condom are 1 out of 10. The problem is that HIV, unlike pregnancy, can strike each and every day of the month. If condoms failed 10 percent of the time for pregnancy, how often must and do they fail for HIV when infection is possible any day, any time?

Is this just a scare tactic, manipulating the statistics to motivate you to abstinence? No. Research the facts yourself. The numbers may vary from study to study, but today no medical authorities dispute that truly safe sex is *impossible* apart from abstinence. To understand condoms and their chemical makeup is to understand why these are not manipulated numbers.

Condoms are inherently flawed. Condoms are made of rubber polymers that have gaps and tears in any sample of rubber material. Are the gaps and tears in the rubber common? No, but when you are talking about HIV and other STDs, who wants to take a chance? Take the natural flaws of rubber and add to the equation the physical nature of sexual activity. Even if a condom did not fail on its own occasionally, the sometimes rough experiences between partners can stretch and strain the rubber polymers, allowing fluid to slip through.

This is still not the most sobering statistic about HIV and condoms. Remember that couples who are 100 percent consistent using condoms in their lovemaking discover that over a six- to twelve-month period the woman can still get pregnant 10 percent or more of the time. That is for pregnancy, the statistics are worse for HIV infection. Not only is the HIV virus able to infect thirty days of the month, unlike the woman's ability to conceive, but also *the HIV virus is smaller than the* standard *holes in latex rubber condoms.*

The molecular structure of rubber polymers, as with any

material, has microscopic holes. The particular size of holes in rubber matter is .5 microns. While material that dense is sufficient to keep sperm from passing through, the HIV virus is only .1 micron, fifty times smaller than the size of the holes in latex condoms. It is quite easy for the condom to prevent some fluids from passing from one partner to another, but it is quite difficult for the condom to prevent the HIV virus from passing through.

That is why officials at the Center for Disease Control in Atlanta and with the World Health Organization are so deeply concerned about the AIDS epidemic. They acknowledge that condoms simply cannot prevent the spread of AIDS.[2]

Condoms do not fit over your mind, heart, and soul. To tell people that using a condom will protect them from the dangers of sex is like telling someone to put on an asbestos glove and then stand for a few moments in a fiery furnace. The hand may not be singed, but the hair and flesh of the rest of the body will be cooked. Likewise, you may not get burned by pregnancy, STDs, or AIDS, but latex won't prevent the mental, emotional, and spiritual burns left by sex.

Your sexuality involves the totality of who you are and the totality of your partner. You can choose to block off your mind or heart or soul during the sexual act, but the bonding aspects (and consequent ripping effects when the relationship terminates) may slip in "under radar." You may not be consciously aware that bonding is occurring, but the condom, which offers a degree of protection from pregnancy and STDs, does not offer a smidgen of protection for your soul.

2. You've Got to Have It

Give me a break. The argument that equates the sex drive with the hunger drive is laughable. Some people think they are actually going to explode if they don't get the sex they need. It's as if they think they have no control over their desires. On the contrary, you have both decisive control over your sexual urges and responsibility before God to commit them to purity. What a tragedy to tell kids and single adults that they are like dogs in heat, rather than humans made in the image of God Himself, with the ability to exercise their own free will.

Your sexual organs do not control you. Rather, you control them. Let me illustrate how you have decisive control over your sexual organs: Imagine you land a date with the most attractive person of the opposite sex. You go out to eat at a nice restaurant, and the two of you are "in the zone," "clicking," etc. Sparks are flying, and you know you have made a connection. You return to your place to watch a movie. Then, all of a sudden, this fantasy date starts coming on to you. Blowing in your ear, kissing your neck—I think you get the picture. Fast-forwarding a few frames, you find yourself naked on the floor, panting with passion, on the verge of having sex, when he or she suddenly pulls away and says, "Wait a minute, I forgot to tell you something . . . I'm HIV positive. But hey, I've got a condom we can use."

Oops! Now what? Are you so helplessly inflamed with passion that you just breathlessly say, "I can't control myself. Go ahead, let's try the condom and just cross our fingers." I don't *think* so! I believe that all of a sudden you're going to discover *instant* self-control. You'll probably feel as if your fantasy lover pulled out a weapon and threatened your life. In this situation the urge to have sex would not overpower your desire to save your own life. The truth is—we *do* have self-control—it's just a matter of whether we want to use it.

3. Sex Equals Intimacy

We have a hard time when we hear pseudocounselors and dating couples define an intimate relationship as "two sexually active people." *Webster's Collegiate Dictionary* defines intimacy as a close, personal relationship marked by affection, love, knowledge of each other's inner character, essential nature or innermost self. If sex equals intimacy, then you could call up a prostitute tonight, have sex, and PRESTO!—you would be intimate.

Many times sex outside of marriage reduces intimacy instead of building it. You say, "But no, I feel intimate with my lover." Perhaps. Sex outside of marriage does create a type of intimacy, but the bonding experience is only a *pseudointimacy*. Sometimes the level of passionate sex is in proportion to the health or stability of the relationship. In other words, it is one way to keep the relationship alive when it seems threatened on all other fronts. It may be the only way to hold a relationship together when in fact it is crumbling.

Real intimacy requires hard work, honesty, mutual self-disclosure, and commitment. And yes, time. Recent media reports of in-depth studies about American sexuality bear this out: couples who have been married for many years record the highest levels for intimacy, happiness, and dynamic sex. Why? Because the real deal takes work and time, and the fruit of that real intimacy is more awesome and indescribable than the pleasure attained by the best bedroom jocks of the casual sex scene.

4. If You Are in Love, It's Okay

Tears poured down the face of a twenty-five-year-old single who fell for the oldest line in the book, and lost her virginity. She said, "We were going to get married. We even looked at houses. I'd waited all this time for someone special and for marriage. Now it's gone."

Some people believe that if you have dated someone for one or two years, and if you are in love, and marriage is a possibility in the future, then sex is okay. Guys dangle the carrot of marriage in front of women as a means of luring them into bed. How many women have shed tears when it was too late, and they had already given in to their urges and his lies? If someone really loves you, he will respect you enough to wait.

True love is an unconditional commitment to an imperfect person. True love is sanctified at the altar, before God and witnesses to sacred vows. Only after you are married, can you say, "I'm in love, it's okay." Apart from the solemn commitment to one another, apart from the sanction of God, sex is never okay. With that lifelong commitment and the sanction of God, sex is a marvelous, incredible gift to be celebrated!

5. You Must Sample the Goods

Some seemingly pragmatic daters believe in a "test drive" before you buy the car. This blunder says great sex = great relationship = happy marriage. If the other partner is sexually incompatible or can't perform in bed, then the "test driver" says *adios*.

Many couples are shocked to discover that what once turned their date on sexually doesn't work so well in the context of marriage. Much of the allure of sex outside of marriage is based on passion, eroticism, and illicitness. Even though many people do not explicitly acknowledge God's view of sex as something to be reserved for marriage, most people still have a sense that there is something wrong, or at least not-as-right, about extramarital sex. That gives sex an allure, an excitement, an element of risk and danger. With those elements added to the experience, of course couples have a sense of heart-pounding, adrenaline-pumped pleasure. Another often overlooked explanation for great sex is the fact that the couple has nothing else going for them in the relationship.

Guess what? If you do marry, the recognized sanction of marriage removes the old allure, excitement, and risk of the illicit sex. You have become so accustomed to the adrenaline rush and the risk of the "forbidden" variety that the "legal" sex you now have in marriage seems boring! Believe me, this is true. We have counseled dozens of married couples who now struggle to maintain excitement in their married sex lives because the dangerous thrill they are used to is gone.

Maximum Sex, God's awesome brand of sex, is based on true relationship intimacy, not illicit thrills. Real intimacy comes not from stealing now what is reserved for later (marriage), but from a host of seemingly nonsexual things: time, respect, honor, commitment, and affection. When sex is based on these things, it is infinitely more fulfilling and exciting than the fleeting moments of "rebellious" sex. Plus—it's guilt free.

6. It's Just a Physical Thing

In the movie *Indecent Proposal*, a billionaire offers another man's wife one million dollars for a one-night stand. The couple desperately needs the money, and while debating the deal, the wife turns to her husband and says, "I'm just going to give him my body, not my soul." What a lie! Sex is a physical thing, but it's preeminently a *soul* thing. Sex connects your soul to the soul of another person like superglue. When the two lovers part ways, there is a ripping and tearing of souls. Every time you have sex and then break up or move on to the next person, a part of your soul breaks off and stays with your former lover.

Try this experiment. Go into the kitchen and open the freezer door. Place your head inside the freezer, then touch your tongue to the metal shelf. Hold it there for a minute, then pull it off quickly. I can almost guarantee that parts of your tongue will remain in the freezer with the ice cream and frozen peas. Likewise, you can't enter a sexual union without scattering a part of your soul and leaving it in the other person. Don't buy into the *Indecent Proposal* lie. Stop fusing your soul to the soul of another by believing that sex is purely physical. It's not.

7. Everybody's Doing It

Granted, we are all susceptible to peer pressure, and it can definitely be difficult to step out of the mainstream and stand on our own. When our friends and the whole culture view us as clueless, hopelessly dull, or just inept, we are tempted to check out the much ballyhooed Nutra-Sex scene.

Everybody does seem to be doing it! From Calvin Klein billboards and countless magazine articles to *Friends* and *Melrose Place*, singles are having sex. Because we are so saturated by the media and coworkers buzz about who's doing what with whom, the legitimacy of extramarital sex is seemingly confirmed everywhere we look.

While pop culture glamorizes sex, it neglects to depict the carnage from casual couplings. It may be hard to swim upstream, and it might seem cool to swim mainstream, but the results are detrimental. "Everybody's doing it" has only resulted in the escalation of STDs, broken hearts, ruptured marriages, unwanted babies, not to mention a whole lot of grief.

SEX ON A DEEPER LEVEL

If you have ever read a book on abstinence or heard a sermon on "The Dangers of Premarital Sex" as a teenager, you probably remember some of the blunders mentioned above. Well, now let's look at sex on a deeper level and see the roots that support these sexual blunders.

The way you express your sexuality and sexual desires is greatly affected by your religion and worldview. If you are a Darwinian evolutionist, unbridled sexual freedom makes perfect sense. Why? Because we are simply naked apes. Somewhat sophisticated and educated, but basically we are naked apes. If you have a sexual desire for someone, then that desire, like hunger, must be satisfied. No wonder teenagers, single adults, and married adults participate in illicit sex—all their lives they've been told that they are nothing more than animals. Unfortunately, millions of Americans are living out the logical implications of Darwinian evolution in their sexual experiences.

But, if you are a Christian or hold to a theistic worldview, then you believe in the concept of a moral law and of a moral Lawgiver. Because this moral Lawgiver, God, clearly states that you should wait until you are married to have sex, you have a choice to make. You can either obey this command or disobey it.

Why do so many professing Christian and theistic singles engage in premarital sex when they know it is clearly violating the law of God? On an unconscious level, they believe sex now is better than sex later. They believe that satisfying their sexual desires now will benefit them more than waiting until they are married.

Faith involves the practice of delayed gratification. Faith

Sex is the belief that God's plan to practice temporary celibacy until marriage will bring maximum results. Sex now is the belief in immediate gratification. It's the belief that the feel-good idol of sex now will bring more pleasure and fulfillment than waiting. We don't disagree that sex now *does* bring pleasure, but ultimately the momentary pleasure fades into lasting pain and guilt.

Hopefully, this is a better way to restate the church's usual party line of "Don't Do It." But hang on, we aren't finished yet. There is a significant, positive reason to adhere to this law to save sex for later.

Why You Should Save Sex for Later

I will never forget a phone call I received from an angry, young, single woman named Nikki. I had given a message on why sex before marriage was not only wrong, but also a stupid choice to make.

"You can't discourage people who want to have sex. You need to teach people to have safe sex and have it with someone they love. I think that's really all that matters," she declared in a defensive tone. After calming her down and explaining the reasonings for my statements, I saw her resolve begin to break, and she eventually opened up to reveal the real issue she was hiding.

"Sex is my addiction, and I'm struggling with intimacy. And I feel the only way I can achieve that is through one-night stands with sex. It's against my beliefs, but I can't stop doing it. It's like a drug. It's scary, you know, it's really scary." She sobbed, and then she hung up the phone.

Many singles are just like Nikki in many ways. They may not be addicted to sex, but they continue to do it out of fear, in a craving for intimacy, even though they know it's against their beliefs. The reason they continue to have sex despite the emptiness, danger, and loneliness is because they do not see a significant reason to wait. Contrary to the mainstream Sex Teaching that sex now will make you feel good, it actually causes us to feel bad about ourselves, destroying our self-esteem, self-respect, and plaguing us with guilt and disappointment.

Carolyn See, in her *Cosmopolitan* article entitled "The New Chastity," puts it where we can see it:

> What does all this mean in a discussion of the new chastity? What it means, I think, is that despite the Pill, legalized abortion and economic freedom, our bodies are trying to tell us something: they don't necessarily want to be tossed around like lost luggage on a round-the-world plane trip. That's why, maybe, after a long night of good times . . . with a Nick Nolte look-alike . . . you go out for coffee in the kitchen, and something, someplace in your body feels like if it could cry, it would cry. It's not your genitalia feeling bad, it may not even be your heart. It's in the vicinity of your lungs, your solar plexus, where some Eastern religions suggest your soul resides. In other words, recreational sex is not soul food.[3]

She continues and begs the question, "Sex is supposed to be fun, freeing . . . yet too many partners can sometimes make you feel disconsolate, unsatisfied. Why are so many young women suddenly swearing off the world of 'junk food' sex?" The answer is that they have found better food for their soul-wholeness.

Making the choice to save sex for later is food for your soul.

It's the choice to be whole again. When you binge on junk food sex, you simply scatter yourself sexually. You devalue yourself, the person you are with, and the sex act itself.

Rick Stedman, in his excellent book *Pure Joy—The Positive Side of Single Sexuality*, says that wholeness can only be achieved by practicing what he calls "temporary celibacy": "Sexual celibacy is the decision that sexuality is of value and personhood is special. When celibate, single adults are saying through their actions, 'I will not reduce my sexuality to a cheap giveaway. I will not pretend it is unimportant or insignificant. It is valuable, and I am valuable. I will assert my worth and value by saving myself until marriage.'"⁴

His premise is that saving sex for later, practicing "temporary celibacy," increases your sense of self-worth and value. Saving sex for later has emotional and spiritual benefits. When you save sex for later, you gain a sense of purity and inner peace. You don't feel scattered or worried, but whole. You no longer have that cheap feeling of being used and the anxiety that you might lose the relationship if you don't respond sexually.

The good news is that you can choose to say no to unhealthy junk food sex, and yes to wholeness. The more you continue to value your body and sexuality by waiting, the more peace and wholeness you will experience.

For too many years, we have looked at celibacy as a negative thing. Let's change this view. The hidden value in waiting until you are married to have sex is the personal peace, wholeness, and joy you will experience for making this decision. If you are a virgin, celebrate your wholeness. Celebrate the fact that you are prized and treasured. Celebrate the value and worth you have because of this healthy choice.

If you have been sexually active, join the Born-Again Virgin

Club. Take a temporary sex break and watch as you regain a sense of wholeness. You may feel that's impossible, like trying to put training wheels back on your bicycle, but it's not. We've worked with hundreds of sexually active singles who have made the commitment to save sex for later and seen God restore what they could never get back.

Following this relationship law will feed your soul with wholeness. Over time, your self-worth and value will increase. You will be able to sleep at peace and no longer worry about what you did last night.

HOW DO YOU SAVE SEX FOR LATER? (IT SEEMS IMPOSSIBLE . . .)

Perhaps you're thinking right now, "okay, enough information, I agree with you. Show me how to make this happen in my life." You are right. Agreeing that saving sex for later is the best choice, the healthy choice, is one thing; but making it happen in real life is another, especially if you have slept around in the past. The following four steps will help you adhere to this commandment:

Step 1: Celebrate Wholeness

There is power in purity. You are making the best choice to save sex for later. You are feeding your mind and body healthy soul food.

What a great feeling it is not to have to worry about the Diet Coke effect. When you drink a Diet Coke, it looks like the real thing, feels like the real thing, and tastes like the real thing for a while. Soon the aftertaste shouts to your mouth, "This isn't the real thing!"

It's the same thing with sex. The aftertaste says, "This isn't the real thing." The aftertaste involves feelings of guilt, shame, and doubt.

When you are whole, you don't have to worry about the aftertaste because it's not there. You don't have to experience the feelings of being scattered and disconnected because you are feeling complete.

Don't just be a wimp about it. Celebrate it. Celebrate the value you have to yourself, to God, and to others. Celebrate the power you feel by saying no to instant gratification and yes to delayed gratification.

We know many singles who are overflowing with joy in their decision to choose wholeness. Rick, after sleeping around for nine years, finally saw the value in celibacy and in saving sex for later. He says his conscience is clean and his life is in new order after four years of "temporary celibacy."

The first step in saving sex for later is realizing you are making the best choice and then celebrating that choice.

Step 2: Receive Forgiveness

It's difficult to celebrate wholeness if you feel unforgiven. We all need healing in the sexual arena.

One of the most powerful ways to experience real forgiveness is to observe how Jesus Christ handled people who were caught in the web of sexual promiscuity.

When He met a woman at the well who had been divorced four times and was currently shacking up with someone, He didn't condemn her. He didn't condone her actions either, but instead shared with her where to find living water.

When some religious fundamentalists caught a woman in the very act of adultery and threw her naked into the dirty streets to be stoned to death, Jesus didn't join them. Instead, He stooped down and drew in the sand, before rising, to say,

"He who has never messed up, throw the first rock" (John 8:7). Everyone backed off, leaving Jesus with the frightened woman. He said, "Where are your accusers? I don't condemn you, either. You are forgiven. Go and lead a righteous life."

When a prostitute poured out her perfume on Jesus' feet in the middle of a Bible study, what did He do? He forgave her and said to the judgmental people looking on, "Therefore I tell you her many sins have been forgiven for she loved much. But he who has been forgiven little loves little."

You can experience that same kind of forgiveness by first acknowledging that you messed up. Just tell God how you feel about your sexual past. Confess how you devalued yourself by scattering yourself sexually. Receive His forgiveness. If the God who made you and placed value on you says, "You are forgiven, you are whole," then what do you have to fear or dread?

The longer you practice saving sex for later and renewing your mind with God's forgiveness, the more forgiven you will feel. It often takes time for our hearts and emotions to catch up with what our minds know to be true. Celebrating wholeness and receiving forgiveness are the initial two steps in this process.

Step 3: Set Clear Boundaries

The most effective way to maintain your wholeness and purity is to set clear boundaries.

After being burned by some of the sexual blunders, Paul decided to do things differently this time. In the past he had sex with every girl he dated, leaving him feeling empty and ruining the relationships.

As a result he made a pact never to sleep with another woman until he was married. By making the decision before he entered the relationship, he set himself up for success.

When he met the woman of his dreams, he told her his commitment to save sex for marriage. When their relationship passed the friendship-only stage, they sat down together, and wrote out their commitment to maintain their purity. They wrote out in detail the limits of their physical contact. Today, Paul and Stephanie are happily married, and blessed because they maintained their value and personal integrity.

Step 4: Stay Accountable

It's nearly impossible to keep your commitment to purity without the help of friends. Having a group of same-sex friends that you meet with at least twice a month will make a radical difference in your life. This gives you the opportunity to encourage one another, confess your weaknesses, and just be yourselves.

We can't emphasize enough the importance of getting grouped! We could not face the demands of our lives without the support of friends whom we still meet with on a regular basis. Within this setting you are free to ask any questions, free to be silent, free to get mad.

Staying accountable to a group of friends will give you the support necessary to keep this commitment to save sex for later. Too many times you might feel you are the only person dealing with sexual temptation. Isolation makes you feel guilty, shameful, and helpless. If you have a group of friends, even just one or two people, to open up with, you'll find that everyone tends to struggle with the same issues.

Take the four-step approach to saving sex for later. Celebrate wholeness. Receive forgiveness. Set boundaries. Stay accountable.

CONSEQUENCES OF BREAKING THIS COMMANDMENT

- You are at risk of contracting an STD or becoming pregnant.
- You will experience momentary gratification followed by intense feelings of guilt, shame, and regret.
- You will sacrifice the sense of wholeness and purity that God desires for you to have.
- You will tarnish the experience of sex as it's intended once you're with your future husband or wife.

BENEFITS OF KEEPING THIS COMMANDMENT

- You will experience maximum wholeness and a healthy sense of self-respect.
- You will have healthier more fulfilling dating relationships built on foundations that last.
- You will enjoy sex inside of marriage the way God intended it to be.

HELP FOR YOU WHO HAVE BROKEN THIS COMMANDMENT

- Make a commitment to become a "born-again virgin" and to save sex until you are married.
- Confess your past mistakes and receive the grace and forgiveness of God.
- Set clear boundaries for physical intimacy before you get involved in another relationship.

Commandment Seven

тноu sнаlt
not play
нouse

Recently, I (Ben) was purchasing new eyeglasses, and the saleswoman asked me about my vocation. Soon the store owner and several customers crowded around me asking questions about my life, marriage, and dating. One customer, a twenty-six-year-old woman, started sharing a little bit about her life and mentioned that she was divorced. After listening to her story, I asked her, "Having been married and divorced, if you had to do it over again, what would you do differently?"

Without hesitating she replied, "I would first live together with him before I would ever consider marriage." I said, "Are you sure?" She responded, "Yes, I'm certain. If I had the chance to do it all over again, I would definitely live together with my future husband."

According to recent polls, her view represents the majority opinion of singles in America. An NBC News poll discovered that 66 percent of young people ages 18 to 32 believe that you should first live together before you get married.[1] The number of couples living together has increased from 523,000 in 1970 to where today there are some 3.7 million couples who are playing house, shacking up out of wedlock. Forty-five percent of all women in the U.S. between the ages of 25 and 34 have at one time lived with someone.[2]

THE LOGIC OF LIVING TOGETHER: THE TEST DRIVE

The logic of living together sounds good on the surface. Some people compare it to buying a car. Imagine going to buy a new car tomorrow. You go into a dealership, and you see this beautiful car and think "This is it!" The look, the gadgets, and the price all seem perfect, and you are swept off your feet. Without further ado you tell the salesman, "I'll take it!"

Is that reality? No way! First you want to take this "perfect car" on a test drive. This is the logic of living together. If you're going to spend the rest of your life with this person, surely you first want to live together, play house, and find out if you're compatible or not. Millions of singles believe that living together allows you to see your partner's true colors before you get married. This, in turn, helps you to make a better, more informed choice.

WHY DO PEOPLE LIVE TOGETHER?

So does the Test Drive Theory prove true? Does living together better prepare you for marriage than not living together? When is it the right time in the relationship to live together?

I'm a why person. I love to know why. For many years, I've been researching this one question: Why do so many couples live together? Here is a brief summary of some of the so-called reasons I get from cohabitating couples:

1. *Love* - Some say, "Well, we're living together because we want to get to know each other better. We've been dating for a while, we want to take it to the next level, so therefore we moved in." Others claim, "We're living together because we love each other. We really love each other. I have so much love to give, so much love to share. It's all about love."

2. *Finances* - If I had a dime for every couple who told me they were shacking up in order to save money, I would be a millionaire. Their rationale goes something like this: "It just makes financial sense for us to live together. This kind of living arrangement helps us pay the bills and save a little cash for our future."

3. *Practice* - Other couples believe that living together is good practice for the real thing. They say, "One day *we're going to get married*." Their motto is "practice makes perfect." I know of a young lady who has been living with her boyfriend for over nine years. Yes, that's right, *nine years*. You would think that she would grow weary of the practice thing and want to enter the real game.

4. *Engagement* - In this day and age, you are considered a bit odd if you are *not* living together with your future spouse. They say it's all about getting prepared for marriage—decorating the apartment, saving money on the last few months' rent, and besides "we're going to get married anyway."

THE REAL REASONS PEOPLE LIVE TOGETHER

Love, finances, practice, and engagement may be the politically correct reasons couples give for cohabitating, but these are not the real reasons they are playing house. There are four real reasons, some conscious and some subconscious, why couples go for the logic of the Test Drive Theory:

1. Fear

The first reason singles are buying the Test Drive lie is because they are afraid. Teens, twenty-somethings, and thirty-somethings have a fear of divorce. Our country's divorce rate has soared off the charts in the last three decades, with many studies showing that over half of all marriages will end in divorce. Marriage is risky business. Thus, singles are moving in together because deep down inside they are scared spitless of having to endure another hellish divorce.

They don't want to make the same mistake that their parents made. They don't want to go through the pain, rejection, and insecurity all over again. Others have already been married and divorced like the woman I met in the eyeglass store. She said, "I'm not going to go through that again. I'm going to live together first before I ever get married. I don't want to make the same mistake twice."

What is their thinking? "Well, if we live together first, and we're not compatible, if it doesn't work out, then we can 'just slip out the back, Jack, make a new plan, Stan, hop on the bus, Gus, and get yourself free.'" Like Paul Simon sang years ago, no strings attached. Just break up—no big deal.

But is that true? Is that reality? Can couples who live

together, who test drive the car, just slip out the back with no strings attached? I don't think so.

Why? Because sex and cohabitation create a bond, and once they enter a sexual union outside of marriage an emotional, psychological, and spiritual bond is forged. When the couple living together breaks up, and starts living apart, there is a ripping and tearing of their souls emotionally, physically, psychologically, and spiritually.

Consider a young woman named LeAnn. A cute twenty-two-year-old girl, just graduated from college, LeAnn fell in love with a guy as they started dating. After a while, she asked him to live with her, reasoning that if things worked out smoothly they would get married some day.

Two years later, they were still living together with no wedding in sight. And when the Test Drive was over and they decided to have their "no strings attached" breakup, LeAnn's world was rocked. She said, "I was so devastated that I had a complete nervous breakdown. I ended up calling my dad every single day, and crying to him for hours because my life was in such turmoil. I was a complete wreck."

LeAnn's live-in realtionship didn't work, and her parting with her "boyfriend" wasn't as free and easy as she anticipated. The fear of divorce reason ends up with the same result because people who break up after living together feel the same way as people who divorce. Not only are ex–Test Drivers like LeAnn emotionally devastated, they are often caught in financial straits.

2. Sex

The second real reason that people are living together is free sex. There's nothing like convenient sex. Most men, if you surveyed them and asked them, "Why did you really move in?" would reply, "I moved in for sex—when I want it and where I want it." It's that simple.

Sexual activity is dangerous these days with STDs on the prowl, and HIV lying in ambush. Repeatedly health officials say that next to abstinence, monogamous sex is the safest alternative. Marriage is obviously the ideal place for that monogamy, but commitment-phobic men have discovered that they can pilfer the benefits of monogamy without the "curse" of commitment by simply living together.

Men move in for easy sex. I've known a guy for seven years and in this time he's lived with over five different women. He enters the relationship, convinces the girl to move in, and then just dangles the carrot of marriage in her face. They will almost get engaged, almost get married, but something will happen, and he'll back off. Then he pulls out his favorite line: "I really love you, honey. Babe, soon we'll be really doing this thing . . . after I get my degree . . . after I get this raise . . . then we're going to get married. You can bet on that." He probably never will get married, but will continue to scam on new women with his tales of "someday, soon, in the near future."

Ladies, please think about this. Why would a man want to get married if he already has one of the most important things to him? If you're already living together and having sex and things get bad, he can just bail. As Grandma always said, "Why buy the cow when you're getting the milk for free?" What's going to cause enough dissonance for him to want to change, and to go on and propose, and get married? Nothing! He has the ultimate deal: sex without commitment.

I (Ben) was talking with a girl in her early twenties who was living together with a Sugar Daddy. I told her that sex is the only thing that keeps a man interested in a live-in relationship. She said that was a lie. So I challenged her to go home and tell her boyfriend/father figure that she was not going to have sex with him for one month, and to wait and see how long he would stick around. Needless to say, she did not accept my challenge.

3. Manipulation

If guys move in primarily for convenient sex, then women move in often to manipulate the man into marriage. Women will trade sex for the hope that someday they will get married. One study revealed that 70 percent of women moved in with a man with marriage on their minds.[3] (The other 30 percent were in denial!)

For many women, living together is really about auditioning, isn't it? They are auditioning for the role of the bride! They think, "If I treat him kind enough, and make him feel good, and if I give him what he wants, then one day he's going to reward me with a ring, and then we're going to have a marriage, and we're going to live happily ever after." So women try to manipulate the man to achieve their own desires. They use sex to get love and hopefully to get him down the aisle.

That's what happened to Julie. Julie fell in love with James, and they had what seemed to be a great relationship. Over time their relationship became more and more intimate. James had just gone through a divorce, so they started living together, and things just looked great.

Julie said, "Looking back, my whole motive for moving in was to be nice to James. I wanted to do things for him that his wife didn't do. I wanted to provide a safe, secure home, and I wanted to do whatever he wanted, so I never talked about the problems that existed in our relationship. I never talked about some of the things that we were doing that made me feel uncomfortable because I wanted to please him. I just wanted to please him."

Weeks passed . . . months passed . . . years elapsed (three, as a matter of fact), and still no ring. Finally, James came home one day and made the announcement: "I think I need to experience the single life. I've already been married, had kids, and right after the divorce we moved in. I need some space. I need to date around and feel what it's like to be really single again."

Their long Test Drive was over. Julie was crushed. She failed to win the role of the bride. And to add to her pain, three weeks after their breakup, she discovered that James had been sleeping with one of her closest friends, and she was pregnant.

Julie, like so many women, tried to manipulate and control, and gave James no conceivable reason to want to leave. However, her manipulation plot failed, and she became a crash dummy from a cruel Test Drive.

4. Immaturity

The fourth underlying reason that people live together is basically immaturity. It's an immature decision to live together before you get married. Why? To build a lasting relationship it takes time, energy, and sacrifice. People who live together before marriage are basically saying, "I want the goodies of marriage without the sacrifice. I want to feel good right now, no matter what." It's like the child who demands his dessert before dinner. It's a basic inability to delay gratification.

That's so childish. People who are living together possess the infantile mentality that is asking this question throughout the Test Drive: "Does this live-in situation feel good every day?" And the other party is working his tail off to be sure that it is feeling good for that person.

Here's the problem with the immaturity-driven desire for

the ultimate "feel good everyday" relationship: What if they actually get married? Their negative feelings have been suppressed to some degree, they have walked on eggshells just to make each other "feel good." Then BOOM, they get married. Guess what? *Marriage doesn't feel good everyday.* Marriage is based on commitment, not feelings. The last time I checked, marriage is for better or for worse, for richer or poorer, in sickness and in health, till death do us part. I read nothing in the wedding vows that talks about feeling good every day as the basis of commitment. It's no wonder that living together is such a poor tester for marriage. It's no wonder that couples who play house are three times more likely to divorce during the first two years of marriage than couples who do not live together.

Some people ask, "What's the big difference between living together and marriage?" That's easy, *commitment.* Commitment, for life. If a person is unwilling to make a commitment to delay gratification, how is that person going to be able to make the same commitment once he gets married?

Dr. Harold Ivan Smith says,

> The transitory, nonbinding nature of a live-in relationship also breeds all kinds of questions: Will he still be there when I get home? What will it take to push her over the edge? What will I do if I find myself suddenly alone? Is he seeing anyone else on the side? . . . A live-in relationship may seem like a simple (and financially attractive) solution to the need for intimacy, but it tends to destroy the things that make intimacy possible: commitment, trust, and vulnerability to another person."[3]

Many times couples will say, "We're living together because we're ready for this kind of commitment." But really, when you look at the situation, *there's absolutely no commitment.* The only thing a Test Driver is committed to is: 1) to stay in the relationship until someone else better comes along, 2) to stay in the relationship until the sexual aspect no longer excites him or her anymore, 3) to stay in the relationship until problems occur. The only commitment in a live-in situation is a commitment to stay until one or the other parties doesn't have a commitment. How's that for some whacked-out logic?

DOES LIVING TOGETHER WORK?

Is living together working? Is playing house adequately preparing people for marriage?

No. According to many recent studies, living together before marriage is detrimental to a marriage relationship.

- Fact #1 - The *Houston Chronicle* reports that couples who live together have an *80 percent greater chance of getting a divorce than those who don't.*[4] Playing house, which is all living together really is, is like playing Russian roulette with your relationship. Except, instead of putting one bullet in the six chambers of the revolver, you're putting four bullets in. Spin the revolver, take your chances . . . and experience relational suicide.

- Fact #2 - A Washington State researcher discovered that women who cohabitate are twice as likely to experience domestic violence than married women. The National Center for Mental Health revealed that cohabitating women have four times, *four times*, higher incidence of depression than married women, two times greater than unmarried women.[5]

- Fact #3 - In one survey of over one hundred couples who lived together, 71 percent of the women said they would not live-in again.[6]

When are we going to wake up and realize "it isn't working"? Not only does living together not prepare you for marriage, it actually works against you, eroding the foundation of trust and respect.

LIVING TOGETHER SENDS A DOUBLE MESSAGE

Dr. Roger Hillerstorm in his insightful book *Intimate Deception*, says that "trying to experience marriage without a lifetime commitment is like going to a doughnut shop to buy your meals. You can fill your stomach, but eventually you'll die of malnutrition."[7]

He explains how couples who are living together are sending a double message to each other. A double message is when two opposite messages are being communicated at the same time.

Picture two people who are dating and feeling romantic emotions. George tells Jenny that he's not ready for marriage but that he wants to take the Test Drive of living together. One message he is sending is "I love you and want to get to know you on a deeper level." Simultaneously, he is sending another message to her, through his actions of not fully committing, which says, "I don't want to get too close, and if things get too tough I'll just have to leave." Throughout the Test Drive, George has his eye on the back door, which is another *big* difference between cohabitating and marriage. In marriage, there is no back door, you can't just conveniently walk out with no strings attached.

Jenny sees George looking at the back door during their relationship and realizes she has nothing—no security, no real commitment. Their relationship is only as good as the last romp in the sack.

Even if they get married, the foundation of their relationship is weak and fuzzy because of the nonverbal double messages communicated throughout their courtship. Cracks in their foundations that they built in their Test Drive days come up in their marriage, and increasingly spread. Little issues like cleanliness, spending patterns, and sexual preference, which were not big deals during their live-in relationship because they could always slip out the back door, become huge, monumental issues in their marriage. They find each other screaming at one another from the top of their lungs, "Change or else . . ." Instead of a foundation of trust and respect, they have built a foundation of disrespect and doubt. The cracks become canyons, and the whole castle of their marriage crumbles into an abyss of selfish doubt and suspicion.

WHAT ARE THE PRACTICAL ALTERNATIVES TO LIVING TOGETHER?

If you are living together right now, let me give you a word of counsel: Stop having sex and move out. If you're serious about getting married, if you're serious about having a successful relationship, the best move you can make is to move out.

Living together and having sex without the lifelong commitment of marriage covers a multitude of flaws. It clouds the

issue. How can you tell if the person has the essential character qualities needed to make a relationship work when you're
having sex or auditioning for the part of the bride? Why subject yourself to usury, insecurity, depression, and possibly
domestic violence?

The solution is so simple: move out. Move into a different
residence if you're serious about getting married to the person
you are living with. Whenever I counsel a couple who is about
to get married and they are living together, I always explain to
them why they must move out before the wedding. Their usual
response is, "There is no way we can do that. She has no place
to live, we can't get a lease in this short of notice, yada, yada,
yada . . ." It's at that time I suggest that they can move into my
house until the wedding. That shuts them up quickly and
allows us to get down to the real reason they are doing it.

If you are engaged and living in the same residence, then
why in the world do you want to have a church wedding? Why
do you want to wear a white wedding dress? Do you want the
minister to ask God to bless a union and commitment that has
already taken place? Why not change your marriage vows like
my friend Rick Stedman suggests:

- "Dearly beloved, we are gathered here today to witness
  what has already taken place . . ."
- "Who has given away this woman a few months ago to be
  married to this man?"
- "Did you take this woman to be your wife . . ."
- "Did you take this man to be your husband . . ."
- "You may kiss your bride again . . ."
- "I now pronounce legally what has already happened
  physically months ago . . ."[8]

Listen, you don't have to become another statistic. You don't have to become another crash dummy on an ill-fated Test Drive. Do yourself, and your partner, a favor and move out, if you are serious about doing the right thing. If you really want to test your compatibility, then get some preengagement counseling. Take the new *Enrich and Grow* inventory, which has been an accurate predictor of couples' compatibility.

One enlightened ex-Test Driver said, "When you get your eyesight back, it hurts like hell." Don't be blinded by the sex and pseudosecurity of a live-in lover. I have so many former cohabitating couples come back to me and say, "Thanks, thanks for telling us the truth."

CONSEQUENCES OF BREAKING THIS COMMANDMENT

- You have a much greater chance of getting a divorce than couples who don't live together.
- You delay the need for marriage by giving a man the ultimate deal—sex without commitment.
- You are more susceptible to domestic violence.
- You are more likely to experience depression than married women.

BENEFITS OF KEEPING THIS COMMANDMENT

- You are practicing self-control, which is a critical character quality for a lasting relationship.
- You are building a healthy foundation of trust and respect.

- You can sleep at night without worrying about an unexpected pregnancy or sexually transmitted disease.

- You will feel more secure in your dating relationships because you can build solid commitments.

HeLp foR you wHo Have BRoken tHis commanDment

- Move out now.

- Confess that what you did was wrong and stupid.

- Receive God's forgiveness and make a decision not to repeat the same mistake.

- If you think this relationship is worth continuing, get some preengagement counseling.

тhou shalt fight fairly

MARK: "What's wrong?"

JILL: [tearful] "We need to talk."

MARK: [annoyed] "What's there to talk about?"

JILL: [sobbing] "It's us. It's our relationship. We don't spend enough time together anymore."

MARK: "Are you crazy? We always spend time together. It's all we do."

JILL: "All you want to do is play golf with the guys, and when we are together, you don't tell me what's going on—you're in your shell."

MARK: [helpless] "Here we go again. You're getting all emotional over nothing. I can't take this. I'm out of here."

JILL: "See? You are so incredibly insensitive. Why don't you ever want to talk?"

Jealousy. Hurt. Accusation. Defensiveness. Insult. Withdrawal. All the ingredients of a good old-fashioned lover's quarrel. Wouldn't you agree? Fighting in relationships is as predictable as the sun's persistent dawn in the east. When one considers the vast differences between men and women in terms of their needs and desires, one easily understands the potential for conflict. As long as men and women engage in the great dance of relationships, conflict will ensue. In fact, conflict is normal, natural, and inevitable.

However, there are definitely right and wrong ways to handle our disagreements with each other. This skill of conflict management, what we call fighting fairly, *must* be a part of your repertoire before entering into marriage. New research in the area of marriage and divorce by Dr. John Gottman and Howard Markman, et al., reveals that neither money, sexual difficulty, or lack of communication necessarily account for divorce. Rather, one of the best predictors of couples' success in marriage is simply how they handle conflict.[1]

In other words, even successful couples have disagreements and difficulties about these issues, but how they negotiate their differences through healthy conflict resolution determines whether or not they stay together. All couples have conflict; some handle it poorly and crater, and others handle it healthily and thrive. Our goal is to help you identify the common mistakes that couples make while fighting and discover techniques for fair fighting, that is, healthy conflict resolution.

THERE ARE NO FREE BITES

Some things just don't make sense. Have you heard about New York's "dog bite" law? Apparently, if you attempt to sue the owner of a dog who has bitten you, you might lose. The law states that in order to collect for damages in a dog bite case, a dog must have a vicious propensity (i.e., history of biting). That means, if you're a dog, you get one free bite! Well, in the world of relationships, every bite counts; you pay for it one way or another. Every insult will damage the relationship. Any act of aggression (including biting) will weaken your foundation. Every defensive maneuver will impede growth. Any unhealthy response to conflict will negatively affect your relationship. Below is a list of our version of the four most harmful responses to conflict: avoidance, defensiveness, invalidation, and intensification.

TOP FOUR HARMFUL RESPONSES TO CONFLICT

1. Peace at All Costs (Avoidance)

One way to handle conflict is simply by avoidance. That is to say, some deal with it by not dealing with it at all. Some believe that conflict is bad, and that no benefit arises through the struggle of trying to resolve differences. Sometimes we see couples who refuse to admit to conflict or disagreement, either because they're deep in denial or because they're being dishonest. Most often denial arises in premarriage counseling, the couple proclaiming, "We've never had a fight" as though they deserve a medal. There is nothing admirable about this.

However, the more common dynamic is where one partner is the avoider, predictably withdrawing at the onset of any problem. The avoider may tune out, shut down, or literally leave your presence. The danger, of course, in these avoidant responses is the tendency to stuff anger and build resentment, which only intensifies as the avoidance continues throughout the relationship. Issues are never resolved, and therefore growth cannot be possible.

This flawed relationship perspective brings to mind the

famous "Peace at Any Price" policy of British Prime Minister Neville Chamberlain. Chamberlain had the misfortune of serving as Prime Minister when Adolf Hitler rose to power in Nazi Germany. Chamberlain abhorred conflict, and the defiant Hitler had him fit to be tied. Master avoider that he was, Chamberlain advocated the practice of appeasing Hitler, i.e., he just denied there was any problem and let Hitler gobble up cities and countries of Europe.

The consequences of "Peace at Any Price" appeasement were the horrendously pricey horrors of World War II. By engaging Hitler, by confronting the real problems, Chamberlain could have saved the world from Nazi evil. However, by sticking his head in the sand, by denying conflict, Chamberlain allowed a small-town bully to become a monster whose name is synonymous with evil.

While the consequences of avoidance in dating don't precipitate world wars, they can ultimately wreak havoc in relationships. It is crucial that we abandon Chamberlain-like appeasement in favor of honest, healthy engagement with problems.

2. Win/Lose (Defensiveness)

The second harmful response to conflict is the tendency to view it as a win/lose situation. Such people usually approach any confrontation or disagreement as an attack, and therefore they assume a defensive posture. The major problem with this approach is that a person can't possibly hear one's partner, empathize with his or her needs, and meaningfully convey that one has heard the other when the person is engaged in frenetic self-defense. Think about it: when you are confronted by your partner, and your focus is on *your* response, *your* perspective, and *your* next strategic move, you can't really hear your partner. Real listening—which means treating your partner with basic dignity—requires seeking first to understand him or her and only then trying to be understood (we'll look at this more in-depth later in the chapter). Defensiveness is really a waste of energy and time, because you can't move forward. Handling conflict is not a win/lose proposition, but rather a team effort, and a chance to grow.

3. You Don't Count (Invalidation)

In the book *Fighting for Your Marriage* Howard Markman et al. define invalidation as "a pattern in which one partner subtly or directly puts down the thoughts, feelings, or character of the other."[2] They go on to express that this is not just disagreeing with your partner, or not liking something he or she has done. It's a form of disregard, disrespect, and insensitivity. Statements such as, "You're overreacting," "You don't feel that way," and "If you think that, then you are stupid" are all prime examples of invalidation. Who can really judge "overreaction"? How can you tell someone what he is feeling? Invalidation always includes an element of judgment, often with some form of disdain. Needless to say, there is no place for this in a relationship.

4. All-Out War (Intensification)

This final response to conflict is a pattern of aggressive fighting, with increasing intensity that often leads to an out-of-control situation. Usually verbal in nature, the fighting is really just a yelling match in which the object of the "game" is to yell the loudest. This is probably the most damaging of all the unhealthy fighting tactics. All-out war can include insults, criticism, name-calling, and physical violence. It is probably the most damaging of all the unhealthy fighting tactics because cruel things are said and done that can never be taken back.

Nobody sets out to get married in order to resolve conflict. We get married with the hopeful anticipation of happiness, harmony, unity, and intimacy. Subsequently, most couples rarely even consider the issue of conflict resolution, much less are they willing to put energy into developing this skill. However, once you enter the marriage arena, it becomes a high priority. I recently attended a rehearsal dinner where the bride and groom were being toasted (and, in some cases, roasted) by their friends. It was interesting to note that, without exception, every remark made by one of the married friends included some underlying theme of marital conflict.

Five Fair-Fighting Techniques

We are well aware of the prevailing attitude about communication and conflict resolution—stretch, yawn, ho-hum, boring. Admittedly, it's not as exciting an issue as money or sex. Still, there is simply no way to get around the necessity of having good skills in this area. We want you to have the five crucial skills for dealing with conflict. These are not mere suggestions or recommendations. These must be utilized for success. Take a look at these five fair-fighting tactics.

1. Dial Down

This is our way of saying that you must calm down before you can expect to communicate with your partner. No one wants to discuss issues or differences when they are feeling attacked by you. So often we try to deal with conflict when we are charged up with anger. Don't buy in to the myth that states you should "seize the moment" while you are good and angry to discuss your concerns. This is a recipe for disaster. Rather, we strongly encourage you to get hold of yourself and take time out to consider what you really need to express, and the most respectful way to express it to your partner.

We're talking about much more than the "step back and count to ten" exercise that is often suggested. Research indicates that men especially may need a minimum of twenty minutes to allow themselves to calm down (physiologically speaking). Hearts race, breathing quickens, and adrenaline floods the system in anger, and the twenty minutes of cooldown time allows those symptoms to subside. Additionally, utilize the approach of taking a full day to allow the emotions to settle and to provide time to reflect about what is really important. It's amazing how our perspective changes when our anger has dissipated.

2. Set the Tone

The first few minutes of any interaction are critical and set the tone for the rest of the conversation. It's that simple. When you approach your partner in a tender, gentle manner you explicitly communicate a willingness to interact in a gracious, nonthreatening way. This also paves the way for openness and respect, which further enhances the communication process.

3. Shut Up and Listen

When was the last time you had a disagreement and your main focus was on trying to really hear your partner? It's probably been a while. If you're like most people, your natural tendency is to seek to be heard first. You pour all of your energies into explaining your side of the story. In his best-selling book *Seven Habits of Highly Effective People*, Steven Covey revealed the most important principle for effective communicating: Seek first to understand, then to be understood.[3] Covey talks about listening with empathy, listening to your partner with the intent of understanding him or her on a deeper level. To have empathy is to convey that you have a sense for what it's like to walk in another's shoes—that you "get it" in terms of understanding their perspective. Such committed listening also communicates that you respect your partner, and you value what he or she has to say. When you can reflect back to them a sense of understanding, it communicates to them that what they have to say is meaningful, valuable, and important. If you want to blow your partner away next time you have a disagreement, just keep your mouth shut and really seek to understand where your sweetheart is coming from. I guarantee you that if you implement this one principle in your relationships from here on out, you got more than your money's worth!

4. Use "I" Statements

Once you have given your partner a chance to express the other side, and you have genuinely sought to understand your partner first, then it's your turn to communicate your perspective. In order to be effective here, you must stick to "I" statements. Making "I" statements includes the ability to personalize, and own, your perspectives and feelings in such a way that the focus is on you, and not the other person. For example, there is a big difference between saying, "I feel hurt when you show up late for our dates" and the statement, "You make me so angry when you show up late for our dates!" In the first statement, the focus is on how you feel. The second statement puts emphasis on your partner. It sounds more like an accusation and an attack, which only leads to defensiveness. Using "I" statements keeps you from criticizing, labeling, accusing, and attacking.

5. Negotiate and Compromise

Some issues can be resolved merely by talking it out, without having to fix something or negotiate differences. Quite often, after both partners have had the opportunity to hear the other side in a respectful, mature fashion they can just drop the issue. However, there will be times when both partners have expressed their sides and the differences still present a problem that must be solved. For these circumstances, we recommend that everyone have a very specific set of guidelines for working toward negotiation and compromise. While this might sound very rigid and structured, in the real world where you and I live there is just no getting around it. I (Sam) hold out little hope for the idealist who expects to be flexible and spontaneous in his or her approach to solving problems. Previously established guidelines are crucial. From my experience I can strongly attest that it doesn't matter how mature and intellectual you are or how "in love" you may be—*you must have a clear set of rules to solve problems.*

Practically speaking, after you both have had an opportunity to express your desires, needs, feelings, and perspectives about a particular issue, then you move into a problem-solving mode. It is crucial to work together as a team and seek to identify the problem as outside of yourselves (as opposed to seeing your partner as "the problem"). Markman et al. have identified four guidelines for problem solving. We suggest you follow them closely.

1. *Identify the problem.* Ask questions to determine the facts: What movie should we see tonight? You want to watch a romantic movie, and I want to see a shoot-'em-up flick.

2. *List possible solutions.* Anything is fair game at this stage. Throw everything on the wall and see what sticks (also called "brainstorming"). No suggestion is too outlandish or inappropriate. This is where creativity really comes in handy. Make sure you come up with an exhaustive list, and be sure to write everything down on paper.

3. *Commit to try one or a combination of possible solutions.* For example: "You pick the movie tonight, and I get to pick it next week. Or you pick the movie, and I choose the restaurant."

4. *Reevaluate your choice at a later time.* We can too easily ignore this critical step in the problem-solving process. You must agree on a time in the future to come back and assess how the "solution" is holding up to reality. In this time, consider whether or not the agreed solution is working for both partners. If not, take the opportunity to try other possible solutions.

There you have it! The five most important skills for communication and effective conflict resolution. Keep in mind our emphasis on "skill." Putting these to use has less to do with personality or intelligence than with determination and perseverance. Anyone can learn these communication skills, but it takes a lot of practice. Finally, we want you to note that even though we refer to this chapter as "Fight Fairly," there is no fighting at all when these skills are put into practice. There is no need to fight because all of a sudden you are communicating as two mature, respectful adults. That is a healthy relationship—conflict recognized, faced, and dealt with in a mature, godly way. Who wouldn't cherish such a relationship?

CONSEQUENCES OF BREAKING THIS COMMANDMENT

- You will experience long-term problems in your relationships because you haven't learned to resolve things.

- You will damage the level of intimacy and communication between you and your partners.

- You will feel higher levels of stress and discontentment (tension).

- You will miss out on learning all there is to know about your partner because you haven't spent enough time *listening*.

BENEFITS OF KEEPING THIS COMMANDMENT

- You will experience a greater level of respect in your relationships.

- You will learn to *resolve* conflict and find solutions rather than seeing the same fights crop up over and over again.

- You will experience greater levels of intimacy in your relationships because you've opened the walls of communication.

- You will feel the freedom to express yourself without fear or apprehension.

Help for you who have broken this commandment

- Realize the conflict resolution errors you have made in the past.
- Be willing to apologize (laying aside pride).
- Think before you speak and choose your words and approach carefully.
- Go into discussions with a spirit of *resolution* not a spirit of just being *right*.

Commandment Nine

thou shalt not ignore warning signs

On the night of April 14, 1912, one of the greatest disasters of all time occurred when the *HMS Titanic*, on her maiden voyage, struck an iceberg and sank in a matter of hours. More than 1,500 men, women, and children were swallowed by the ocean, never to be seen again. Unless you've been living in a cave for the last several years, you probably witnessed the sinking of that famous ship in full cinematic glory at your local movie theater. To date, the movie *Titanic* has been the most successful motion picture in history, grossing well over a billion dollars.

Among many things, the movie underscores the fact that the captain and crew knew in advance that it was too dangerous to be sailing in that region that night. In other words, this tragedy could have been avoided. *Titanic* began receiving radio messages from other ships to lookout for icebergs as early as Friday, April 12. By Sunday, the weather had grown colder, and the warnings were more frequent. Another steamer, only twenty miles away, called to warn that she was stopped and surrounded by ice. Also troubling was the fact the men in the *Titanic's* crow's nest, ordered to look out for ice, were never issued binoculars. In spite of all the warnings and the lack of preparation, *Titanic* continued to cruise full speed ahead that fateful night. Caught up in the excitement of sailing this large, "unsinkable," luxurious ship, the captain failed to heed obvious warning signs along the way.

How many men and women wake up after their honeymoon (or luxury cruise) to the realization that their relationship is already sunk? How many marriages have ended up dead in the water because someone ignored important warning signs and red flags during the dating period? Numerous indicators can warn that a relationship may be heading for the rocks, or at least for some sandbars (frequent conflict over minor issues, a decline in communication), but in this chapter we focus on *seven major warning signs*. These seven signs don't merely suggest problems that need to be worked on at some vague time in the future, they are big red stop signs.

Jenny Jones, Jerry Springer, Oprah—these hosts' shows are about people who ignore relationship warning signs. People who go on talk shows to say things like "My twin sister slept with my fiancé even though he's a transvestite heroin addict" obviously missed major hints of calamity somewhere along the way. As wild and wacky as these TV shows are, some of us can look at incidents in our own relationships and realize that we could easily be fodder for *The Jerry Springer Show*. How often do singles ignore the warning signs that could keep their relationships from becoming talk show material?

We believe that far too many couples are cruising down the church aisles with some awareness of major red flags. More than likely, these red flags are actually one-hundred-foot banners screaming, "GET OUT WHILE YOU CAN!" When you see warning signs, red flags, or something else that makes you say "Uh-oh," we suggest that you deal with them immediately. Here is a list of the seven warning signs you can't afford to ignore.

THE SEVEN DEADLY SIGNS

Warning! The following comments concerning the seven deadly signs are quite harsh. We are committed to speaking the truth, and we make no apologies for our lack of political correctness. We've seen too many victims of relational Titanics to be blasé. We long for singles to experience relationships that are free of the pain we see in our counseling offices, on the *Single Connection* radio show, and especially on TV talk shows. If it requires saying some hard truths in a sharp manner, so be it. Please understand that we have deep compassion for all the people who struggle with any one or more of the seven deadly signs. Hopefully these words can bring clarity and resolve, which lead to healing.

One more thing: *Our hope is that if you have any of these seven problems, you will find help immediately by sharing with someone you trust, and then by seeking professional help.*

1. Abuse

One of the most destructive warnings signs for a relationship is any form of abuse. Statistics reveal that violence and abuse within marriage reach almost epidemic proportions. Sadly, many people don't understand what abuse actually entails. For example, most people think of abuse as only physical contact. However, abuse encompasses a broad range of aggressive behaviors, including physical, verbal, emotional, and sexual behavior. *All* of these forms of abuse can be equally damaging and will threaten the health of any relationship. Are you wondering how to define abuse? Take a look at these definitions Adapted from materials published by the Austin Stress Clinic:

- *Physical abuse* - any use of size, strength, or presence to hurt or control someone.

- *Verbal abuse* - any use of words or voice to control or hurt another person.

- *Emotional abuse* - any action or lack of action meant to control or demean another.

- *Sexual abuse* - any sexual behavior, verbal or physical, engaged in without consent, which may be emotionally or physically harmful.

So while you may know that hitting, kicking, and choking are abusive, did you know that *threats* to hit or harm are also abusive? Are you aware that insults and name-calling qualify as abuse? Have you considered that intense jealousy and manipulation with lies are also abusive? How about criticism, intimidation, and humiliation?

Abuse can take many forms, and sometimes it can even be quite subtle. Regardless of the form that it takes, abuse is *never* justified. There is no rationalization or excuse that could justify abusing another person. *There is no reasonable defense or explanation that can support any form of abuse—ever.* We are always astonished at the efforts to justify abuse. "But he didn't mean it" or "Well, his father was that way; he can't help it" or "Maybe I pushed her to that point, and she just snapped." And the scariest response of all: "It's all right because I know it will never happen again." Don't bet on it!

A woman in her late-twenties came to see me (Sam) for help with her relationship. Her dilemma was in trying to choose between two men who claimed to love her deeply. Her descriptions of these two men revealed they were as different as night and day in terms of their character and the way they treated her. Surprisingly, she was more drawn to the one who was disrespectful and emotionally abusive. When she went out with other men, he responded by becoming violent with her and verbally assaulting her by calling her demeaning names and making accusations about her moral integrity.

Her response was, "I know he loves me because he gets so jealous and angry when I'm with someone else. I don't much like the names he calls me, but at least it shows he cares." What? He cares? He loves you? This has nothing to do with love!

This woman was so confused by her emotions and dazzled by the man's sweet talking during the makeup process, that she couldn't recognize the severe abuse that was taking place against her. After some intensive counseling, she was able to discover the truth about real love and respect, and she learned to set healthy boundaries for herself. She later acknowledged, "I had a sense that something wasn't right, but I just needed to hear it from someone else." Maybe you too have a gut sense that your relationship is abusive, and you just need permission to do something about it.

So what do you do if you discover there is abuse in your relationship? Our advice is to give your partner one more kiss—a kiss good-bye. Get out of an abusive relationship now and ask questions later. You may be thinking, *Well, that sounds pretty harsh and unforgiving.* Yes, it is harsh, but that is your best response. Oh, eventually you do need to forgive, but that doesn't mean you have to allow this person access to your life until he or she has demonstrated genuine sorrow and deep, long-lasting change. We feel very strongly about the need to deal with this immediately. At the very least, you should insist that the person get help right away and suspend the relationship until he or she has been through some form of treatment and healing to ensure that it will never happen again. Remember, rehabilitation and proof of lasting change may take a long time.

Abuse of this kind involves two parties, right? One to be abusive and the one to be abused. Take away either person, and the abuse isn't happening anymore. If you find yourself frequently drawn to abusive people, refer back to the First Commandment: Thou Shalt Get a Life. Sometimes people (more often women) are attracted to romantic partners, not despite their abusive tendencies, but because of them. These women may have low self-esteem and feel an unconscious need to be punished somehow. To be sure, there are a lot of different issues involved in low self-esteem. But one way to increase self-esteem, and make yourself less vulnerable to abuse, is to make your own life productive and fulfilling before you ever look for someone to share it with. You'll find that there is a direct correlation between the quality of life you live all by yourself and the quality of the people you end up with later. This advice holds true for the other Seven Deadly Signs, too, such as addictions and infidelity.

2. Addictions

By its very nature, an addiction is a powerful, habitual form of behavior that cannot be overcome merely by a decision to stop. I guess it could be argued that we all have an addiction to something, whether it be caffeine, computers, cars, or more dangerous substances like alcohol, marijuana, or cocaine. For our purposes, let's focus on the latter group of addictions, the relationship destroyers—alcohol and drugs (including prescription drugs).

Essentially, when you are in a relationship with an addict, you are dealing with someone who is enslaved to his addiction. That means he is in bondage to his drug of choice. He is controlled by a substance. Therefore, the addict is not available to have a healthy relationship. Period. You see, trying to maintain a relationship with someone who has an addiction is like trying to make a "threesome" work. Your partner is having an affair with his drug of choice, and that substance will always be the priority. Would you allow yourself to be in a relationship with someone who had "others on the side"? Of course not! It is no different when you are dealing with addictions. What's more, if you want to continue in a relationship with an addict, you must be willing to deal with some pretty sour characteristics. Here is just a taste of what you can look forward to: denial; emotional unavailability or numbness; controlling, obsessed, or preoccupied behavior; unpredictability; inconsistency; irresponsibility; blaming; rationalization; self-deception; and lying, just to name a few. Most of these characteristics involve the need to maintain the addictive behavior at all costs. That is why you will always be second priority.

How do you define an addict? We define an addict based on one or a combination of these three signs: (1) anyone who demonstrates a pattern of using a substance that alters chemistry or mood, (2) anyone who spends a significant amount of time (daily or even every weekend) acquiring and consuming the drug of choice, and (3) anyone who continues to use in spite of the fact that his or her life is out of control and unmanageable, or the person is experiencing obvious physical or psychological effects (i.e., depression, liver disease, or problems at work).

The worst thing you can do for yourself and the addict is to do nothing and hope it goes away. You become part of the problem, and potentially a "coaddict" as the enabler of this behavior. We recommend that you confront this behavior head on. Try the tough love approach. Insist that your partner get help immediately through some form of recovery, individual counseling, or twelve-step group. If he or she is unwilling to get help right away, or if your partner make excuses, then you *must* get out of the relationship. It is imperative that you stick to your guns on this. Threats to leave without follow-through will do no good. We also recommend that you not even consider going back until the person has freedom from the addiction and has dealt with the root cause. Most serious addictions have their basis in deeper emotional issues.

3. Infidelity

If you are in a serious relationship with someone who is or has been unfaithful, we suggest you think twice about continuing it. Here's why. Trust is one of the foundations of a healthy relationship. But when there is unfaithfulness or infidelity, especially in the early stages of a relationship, then trust is shattered before it is even fully established. When unfaithfulness occurs in the early stages of a relationship, it is rare for any couple to fully recover from this betrayal. If you can't begin a marriage with trust, you have nothing to build from. You have nowhere to go. It's pretty much over at that point.

Not too long ago, William came into my office to discuss his grief over the loss of his girlfriend of two years. I was quite sympathetic until he admitted that she dumped him because he had cheated on two separate occasions. He exclaimed,

"They were innocent slips. There was never anything between us, just one-night stands."

Sadly, William was more concerned with the "unjust" breakup than with his own problem of infidelity. Trust had been broken, and it was obvious that his girlfriend was not willing to invest the time and energy into working on rebuilding the trust and restoring the relationship. Can you really blame her? I still have empathy for William but for different reasons. It's clear that he has a bigger problem than the grief surrounding his breakup. If someone is unfaithful to you while you are dating him, what would keep him from doing this again? If he cheats on you before marriage, what guarantee is there that it wouldn't occur after marriage? A piece of paper? I don't think so. You see, the problem of unfaithfulness is a much deeper issue of character, and possibly much more. This is typically not something you can change overnight. So if this has occurred in your relationship, and you are wrestling with what to do, consider the fact that you deserve better, and give it the old *hasta la vista*, baby.

By the way, our advice about infidelity cuts both ways: if you find that you're constantly tempted by others even though you "love" the one you're with, think twice about whether you are ready to be in a relationship.

4. Irresponsibility and Immaturity (The Peter Pan)

To be in love with a Peter Pan is not necessarily to be in love with someone whose daily attire is a green hat and pointy green shoes, although if this were true you should be worried. No, the hallmark of the Peter Pan is the manifestation of irresponsibility and immaturity. When you find yourself with someone who hasn't quite grown up, you should consider this a serious warning sign. You need to start asking yourself a lot of questions before you get too deep in the relationship.

Particularly, does this person demonstrate irresponsibility in crucial areas such as life direction, self-care, financial management, relationships, and vocation? Now, please don't misunderstand us. We aren't talking about someone who occasionally misplaces his car keys and forgets to take out the trash, nor someone who has a playfulness about him. *What you should be concerned about is dating someone with a pervasive pattern of immaturity or irresponsibility*. If this is going on, your sweetheart is trying to tell you something, namely, "I don't want to grow up. Will you please take care of me?"

Characteristics to watch out for:

- Lacks goals, direction, and purpose for life
- Doesn't take care of self (poor hygiene)
- Is indecisive about many things—even trivial decisions
- Constantly puts off doing things until the last minute (procrastinates)
- Is often late for important engagements
- Regularly misplaces significant personal items like a checkbook or wallet
- Waits for others to initiate social activity or relationships
- Has difficulty keeping a job for a reasonable length of time
- Has poor credit history
- Keeps house or apartment looking like a disaster
- Forgets important dates
- Has careless spending habits

- Constantly bounces checks or is overdrawn at his bank
- Often borrows money (mooches) from others

People with a pattern of the above characteristics are generally unreliable, unmotivated, and unsure of themselves. For whatever reason, these folks haven't grown up (don't worry about *why* this is so, let their therapist figure that one out). Typically, they are often hinting that they need to take a long trip to Colorado or Europe to "find themselves." You don't want to get wrapped up in a relationship with this kind of person, unless they do actually find themselves! If you are already involved with someone described above, take heed and remember you may be flirting with one of the seven deadly signs.

5. No Physical/Sexual Attraction

Surprisingly, one of the more common questions we are asked is, "What if you aren't attracted to your partner on a physical level?" What can we say? If there is nothing there, what are you doing in this relationship? Certainly this isn't the most important aspect of a relationship and it alone will not sustain a healthy relationship, but it is very important nonetheless.

When it comes to physical attraction and that intangible quality called chemistry we have no formulas to offer. There are no "Ten Steps to Developing Chemistry" with your partner. You either have it or you don't. And it is not too likely that you will ever grow into it or somehow be successful at making it happen. Sorry, but we just believe that any great relationship has some element of chemistry. Precisely how much is not for us to say. It is true that some start out a relationship as friends and there is little attraction to begin with. But often as the relationship develops and people get closer the attraction begins to emerge. That's great! We are all for that. What we are concerned with here is the relationship that has nothing from the very beginning and still nothing after many months or even years of trying to make it happen.

6. Emotional Baggage

The sixth deadly sign is what we call emotional baggage. It is the man or woman who carries significant, unresolved emotional or psychological baggage from their past that interferes with normal, healthy relational functioning. From the outset we want to establish the fact that we all have some emotional baggage from the past. So we are not saying you should only find someone who is free of all emotional issues (it's not going to happen in this lifetime). We are saying that you must beware of those who have little or no insight into their issues, and subsequently have never resolved them, or have never even begun the process of working on them.

Melvin was a tall, dark, handsome man in his mid-thirties. An investment banker with a nice six-figure income and a shiny, silver Porsche, he was active in his church, had an outgoing personality, and seemed to be liked by everyone. He had it all. He was every woman's dream. Right? Wrong! What you don't know about Melvin is that attached to his shiny, silver Porsche was a U-Haul trailer full of enough emotional baggage to keep the Samsonite corporation in business for years. Through no fault of his own, Melvin was from a dysfunctional home marked by trauma and chaos. He was raised by an alcoholic/rageaholic father who was physically and verbally abusive. His mother was emotionally unavailable, and didn't seem to have a life of her own. She was addicted to prescription drugs and was constantly preoccupied with appeasing Melvin's father, until they divorced midway through Melvin's seventh grade year in school. Melvin became an alcohol and drug user himself by the age of fifteen in order to cope with his pain.

Melvin is someone who represents the sixth deadly sign—not because of what happened to him but because he has never taken the time to acknowledge the hurts, understand the effects, and work toward some form of emotional healing. No doubt there are many who have experienced similar tragedies as mentioned above for whom we have tremendous empathy and respect. The truth we want to drive home is that any one of those traumatic experiences, by itself, is enough to create "emotional baggage" that should be addressed before you can expect to establish a healthy relationship.

"So we all have issues from the past; where do we go from here?" you ask. Remember that your partner's emotional issues only become "baggage" if they are not aware of their issues in the first place, or if they have not begun the process of healing.

One of the more valuable aspects of my (Sam's) training as a psychologist was the requirement to participate in some group therapy and individual counseling. Through these opportunities, I was able to discover certain relational blind spots and uncover some hidden issues that needed to be addressed. Though painful and somewhat arduous, the process of self-discovery and growth proved to be a rewarding experience. When you've got issues, baggage, or childhood wounds, your best response is to face it, acknowledge it, feel it, talk about it, and then do something about it. Don't be afraid to seek professional help, pastoral help, or some other form of support in order to address your issues.

You need to ask yourself three questions about your partner to determine whether or not you are dealing with a warning sign: (1) Does he have a reasonably clear awareness and under-standing of his issues? (2) Does she know how these issues affect her current relationships? and (3) Have these issues been dealt with or is the person actively engaged in healing and recovery?

7. Denial

The seventh and final warning sign comes when you, after reading this chapter and the previous chapters, have an under-standing that there are serious concerns in your relationship, but you can't seem to get out. You know it's wrong, and you're sure nothing will change, but you simply will not heed the warning sign. Or you may find that you have a strong desire to leave, and yet something holds you back. There are others who might consider themselves the exception to the rule, min-imizing, rationalizing, or just flat denying the truth. In any case, if you can identify with any of the above warning signs you are living out the seventh deadly sign. It's as though you're driving down a road in broad daylight. You suddenly notice orange cones, flashing lights, and a sign that says, "BRIDGE OUT, TURN BACK"—but all you can do is speed up. Why are some people drawn in to these kind of relation-ships? Why do others stay in them against their better judg-ment? Here is a list of the top five reasons why people ignore red flags:

1. *It's familiar to them.* Sometimes people get into unhealthy relationships because it is all they know. They are somehow drawn to relationships that are familiar. For example, it is not uncommon for a woman who grew up with an alcoholic father who spent all his money on booze to end up marrying a man who is an alcoholic himself. According to

this theory, this is all that she knows—it's predictable and strangely familiar.

2. *They don't deserve anything better.* Certain people grow up with an incredible sense of inferiority, a lack of self-respect, or guilt that leads to the belief that they deserve nothing but the worst in life. This is often the result of childhood neglect or abuse. Sadly, we've known people, for example, who actually believe they deserve to be hit or demeaned. No matter how much you try to reason with them, they can't intellectualize their way out of it. It requires intensive professional counseling.

3. *It's better than nothing.* Others actually make a conscious decision to stay in a "red flag" relationship because they feel they get something else valuable out of it. They often reason their way around the problem, knowing full well there is a concern, by saying to themselves, "I know this is a serious concern, but I'm willing to take my chances because it's better than being alone." What's the old saying—"Some attention—even if it's negative—is better than none at all." We don't believe anything could be worth the pain that is associated with any of the seven deadly signs.

4. *They have the same problem.* It's hard to judge someone (or identify serious problems) when you've got the same problem. I (Sam) remember working with an engaged couple who both admitted they were daily pot smokers. In spite of my warnings and urgings to address this serious issue, neither one could see any problem with this behavior (massive denial), and hence were incapable of having higher expectations for each other or for the relationship. Needless to say, it wasn't too long after we stopped counseling that I heard their relationship didn't make it. Was I sad about the breakup? Of course. Was I surprised? No.

5. *Fear of the breakup.* Many people stay in sick relationships

against their better judgment due to any number of fears: fear of being alone; fear of the unknown; fear of not finding another partner; fear of the hurt and loss associated with the breakup; and fear that the partner may do something crazy or irrational. Unfortunately, these fears hold a lot of power when they are kept in secret. Fear can lead to paralysis. Thus, it is critical to verbalize your fears to others. Share them with a trusted friend, pastor, or counselor.

Perhaps this chapter seems to reek of doom and gloom to you, what with our dire warnings about all that can go wrong in a relationship. But you don't have to treat these scenarios as your fate—we are making you aware of the warning signs so that you can eventually forge a *healthy* relationship. If you want, try compiling your own list of signs that indicate a relationship is going well. Your own personal list will help you remember exactly what it is that you value in a relationship.

consequences of breaking this commandment

- You risk the possibility of sinking into abusive, unhealthy, and destructive relationships.

- You are at a greater risk of entering an unhappy marriage and becoming another divorce statistic.

- Your self-esteem will be damaged as you persist in relationships that are void of mutual respect.

- You compromise the possibility of finding fulfilling relationships with someone who exhibits character—someone you can respect.

BENEFITS OF KEEPING THIS COMMANDMENT

- You'll avoid the heartache and pain of trying to let go of a dysfunctional, unbalanced relationship.

- You'll avoid the rise of enduring abuse and addiction in your relationships.

- You'll open the possibility of meeting "Mr. Right" instead of "Mr. Right Now" and not compromising what you need and want in a relationship.

- You'll enjoy happier, more fulfilling relationships with people you are compatible with.

HELP FOR YOU WHO HAVE BROKEN THIS COMMANDMENT

- Realize that God wants the very best for you.

- Look at the red flags and decide if they are things you can live with.

- Apply "Band-Aid rip" and then move on!

- Consider the essential character qualities (ECQs) that are important to you and be unwilling to compromise them even if it means remaining single indefinitely.

тhou shalt choose wisely

Do you ever feel like your quest to find The One is like that never-ending search for the Holy Grail? Remember that blockbuster movie *Indiana Jones and the Last Crusade*? Indiana Jones, played by Harrison Ford, and an evil character named Donovan are searching for the Holy Grail, the supposed fountain of youth. At the end of the flick, Indiana and Donovan find the room where the grail is being protected by a seven-hundred-year-old knight. They have to pick the right grail from a selection of about twenty-five. The knight tells them both that if they choose the right grail they will have eternal life. If they choose the wrong grail? Eternal damnation.

Donovan gets his sexy, blonde sidekick to make his choice. She impulsively grabs the most beautiful and shiny of the chalices, and hands it to Donovan. He holds the cup high and says, "Surely this is the cup of the King of kings." He dips the grail into a pool of water and quickly gulps it down. After breathing a sigh of relief, positive that he has chosen the right cup, he notices the reflection of his face in the pool. Suddenly, he begins to age and wrinkle, his hair grows out, and his entire face rots, turns into a skeleton, and explodes across the screen. After Donovan disintegrates before their very eyes, fragmenting into thousands of pieces, the old knight slowly turns to Indiana and the woman and says, "He chose . . . *poorly.*"

How many men and women across the globe have had their hearts and lives torn apart because they chose poorly in the dating process? Why do more than half of all marriages crater in divorce? Why do so many couples divorce each year before they have a chance to celebrate their second wedding anniversary? It's partly because men and women are simply choosing poorly! They're selecting the wrong people to date and then marrying one of them.

You can make a lot of bad decisions in your life and recover. Believe us, we've been there, done that, and have several T-shirts to prove it. You can select the wrong car and trade it in after a few months. You can choose the wrong college and transfer if you don't like it. You can pick the wrong major and revise it later. You can take the wrong job but later land another that you like better. You can make foolish financial decisions and even end up in debt, but you can recover by wising up and paying off those debts. You can relocate to the wrong city, and move to another one that suits you better. All of these decisions may carry some adverse consequences but pale in comparison to the consequences of bad decision making in an intimate relationship: *If you date and then marry the wrong person, you will live with significant, negative, and lasting consequences of that decision for the rest of your life.* This bears repeating: whether or not you stay married, you will live with significant, negative consequences of that decision. If you choose poorly in the dating arena, that choice can affect every area of your life. Our hearts go out to the people whom we talk to every week whose lives have been devastated by a bitter divorce or who feel stuck in a dead marriage because they chose poorly.

ARE YOU MAKING POOR CHOICES?

Donovan made the wrong choice for several reasons: he was impulsive and desperate, he allowed the "sexy blonde" to influence his choice, and, finally, he assumed that his choice was the best based on the external beauty of the chalice. Just as Donovan chose poorly in his quest for the Holy Grail, so do scores of people during their quest for a mate. We have identified four of the more common reasons people tend to make poor choices. Each of these reasons serves to keep people from discerning the true character of those they are dating (which of course is the reason for dating in the first place).

Take a look at these barriers to discerning true character:

1. *First-Available Syndrome*—You are desperate for love, and therefore settle for the first available warm body.

2. *Fooled by the Externals*—You are looking for the wrong things and are thereby fooled by the superficial qualities.

3. *Blinded by Sex*—You are literally incapable of seeing the faults and negative traits in another because of the sexual relationship.

4. *Going Too Fast*—You are in such a big hurry to get married that you miss important road signs along the way.

1. First-Available Syndrome

When you don't know what you are looking for and you are desperate or starved for love, you wind up compromising your standards and settling for the first available warm body. We call this the First-Available Syndrome. Do you ever get ravenously hungry, speed to your favorite restaurant, and breathlessly ask the hostess to seat you? The hostess politely responds, "Do you want smoking, nonsmoking, or first available?" You could care less about secondhand smoke at this point, so you respond, "Please give me *first available!*" Many people are so love hungry that they are willing to take the first available man or woman who comes along. As radio shrink Dr. Laura Schlessinger says, "They become beggars not choosers," in the dating process.

Chad fell into the First-Available Syndrome when he turned thirty-nine. He had lived his life as a bachelor up to this point and decided he was running out of time. He scouted the classified ads, found a woman who sounded reasonably compatible on paper, and married her six months later. He was so intent on finding just about anyone that he never took seriously the fact that she had been married three times before. Unfortunately, this marriage lasted two months. In this case, they both chose poorly. He chose someone with no real understanding of commitment, and she chose someone whose heart was never really in it in the first place. Be a chooser and not a beggar in your relationships. Know what you want, and more importantly, know what you *need* before you ever go out.

2. Fooled by the Externals

Have you ever purchased a used automobile? If your experience is like most folks', as you step onto the lot and begin to talk about the specific things you're looking for, the car salesman starts to drool, especially when you focus on the externals. "I want a red one, with shiny wheels, CD player, sunroof, and leather seats. Hey! There's one over there! Wow, that looks *awesome!*" Many of us have experienced the stomach-churning trauma of bringing home that shiny red beauty, only to find major problems with the engine or some other mechanical failure with no warranty. Chalk up another for the externals. They cry, "Gotcha!" again.

Nearly every week in counseling sessions or on the radio, we ask singles the all-important question: "What are you looking for in a member of the opposite sex?" By far, most people will initially say, "Well, I'm looking for a person with a good personality, someone who is outdoorsy, funny, good-looking, has a great body, money, etc." And they go on and on listing a host of superficial characteristics and personality traits.

We call this the "Cotton Candy" approach. At a fair or circus your attention gets snagged by the cotton candy vendor. Cotton candy looks colorful, beautiful, and like a mountain of sweetness. Then you stuff a wad in your mouth and it just melts away. Oh sure, it's sweet, but you paid $5 for this huge thing that vanishes in seconds, leaving you unsatiated.

Melissa tried the Cotton Candy approach. A banker, she was bowled over by an older man in the industry, a man who had it all. Donald's career had taken off like a rocket, he was already wealthy, and his good looks and charm put the perfect bow on the package. Melissa sailed blissfully through a brief dating stint, dazzled by the externals, and got engaged. Only weeks before the wedding did she see cracks in the facade, and when she looked more closely she discovered a frightening truth. Donald was living a double life—he was a fake. He was selfish and dishonest as could be. His Cotton Candy perfection melted into nothing, and thankfully Melissa discovered this in time to break off the wedding.

Don't get us wrong—personality and common interests are important—but alone they won't build a lasting relationship.

Gazing at the externals may fool you. Psychologist Henry Cloud puts it this way: "What we are attracted to in a person is what we see on the outside, their looks and personality, but what we end up experiencing in a long term relationship is what we cannot see—that's their insides, their character."[1]

3. Blinded by Sex

The Bible says, "Love covers a multitude of sins," but when it comes to dating relationships, sex covers a multitude of flaws. Sex has a way of blinding you from seeing your partner's true colors. We all have "lenses" through which we look at life. These glasses or paradigms filter all data—some stuff gets filtered out, some stuff makes it through. Sex acts as a filter in a dating relationship, filtering out the red flags of another's character and letting only rose-colored data through.

Jonathan called the radio show one night to explain how great his sex life was with his girlfriend before they got married. He complained, "When we finally exchanged vows, she turned into the Wicked Witch—angry, controlling, and demanding." I don't buy it. She didn't change when they got married, I'm sure she was always that way, but he couldn't see it because "the sex was *sooo* good."

Sex is great in the right context (marriage), but in dating relationships sex often clouds the relationship and shuts down communication. Men usually mistake the love-making for intimacy. In other words, they are duped into thinking that sex equals closeness, and therefore there is no need to work at other forms of intimacy (emotional, verbal, or spiritual). Women, on the other hand, have a tendency to confuse sex with commitment. The common misconception is that the man somehow values this relationship as unique and special. A woman will think to herself, *This must really mean love.* Come on women, wake up! Some men will potentially make love with anyone, anyway, anytime, anywhere, for just about any reason under the right circumstances. So, whether it's trading sex for love or love for sex, the sexual relationship gives one a false sense of closeness, and it blinds both parties from seeing the real person they are dating.

4. Going Too Fast

The number-one killer of people on the highway is not alcohol, it's speed. The number-one killer of potentially good relationships is also speed. So many well-meaning singles exceed the *relationship speed limit*. Men and women igniting new relationships often jump on the autobahn, which has no posted speed limit. They zoom off, reveling in the thrills and chills of instant intimacy. However, what they really need is to drive through the school zone first, going slow and getting to know each other. Nearly every time we speak about dating, we emphasize, "Take it slow, take it slow." Tragically, plenty of people ignore the speed limits and hop on the dating autobahn with the Eagles' song "Life in the Fast Lane" blaring in their ears.

Recently a friend of mine "borrowed" a twenty-five-mile-an-hour speed sign so I (Ben) could use it in a speech about the necessity of taking it slowly in relationships. Throughout the talk, I held up the sign or leaned on it and pointed to it continually in order to reinforce this principle. After the session, a girl came up to me a said, "I liked what you had to say and I agree with you, but I don't like to drive slowly in my car or in my relationships." I don't like to drive slowly either, and sometimes it's extremely annoying to pass through a school zone in the morning, especially when you are late for work. But slowing down in the school zone and driving the appropriate speed limit saves lives. So does going slowly in relationships. No matter how much fun it is to put the pedal to the metal, taking it slowly and getting to know the person you are dating can save your relationship.

Brad and Allison put the pedal to the metal during their first date. They swerved onto the relational autobahn, and soon were kissing and caressing and staring dreamily into each other's eyes. Within three weeks Brad was telling his friends that she was the one. The thrills were tangible, and he thought Allison could do no wrong. Still cruising at breakneck speed, they got married, and only months into their marriage did Brad discover that Allison was really not the person he needed in a wife. While neither consider divorce an option, their relationship *now* putters along in the school zone, and the heady days of the autobahn are behind them. A mediocre marriage resulted because they didn't get to know each other slowly, over time, and discover their incompatibility beforehand.

When you zoom through the dating process in an attempt to bond faster than Krazy Glue, you never get to know what the person you are dating is really like. In counseling people who are in a miserable marriage or are walking around wounded from a divorce, we've heard far too many people lament, "If I had just taken the time to know this person, I would never be in this mess."

When you are in too big of a hurry to find your mate for life, you usually settle, minimize your partner's faults, or flat-out deny major problems. Dating is not a race to see who can get to the finish line in the shortest period of time. Dating should be a long-term process of discerning whether or not you are compatible with a person, and whether or not the two of you have what it takes to build a lasting relationship. Make this your motto: "I'd rather be single than settle."

If you desire to make wise dating choices, to know what you want so you don't settle for the "first available," make sure your focus is on the internals (like the Essential Character Qualities you are about to discover), save sex for marriage, and take it slow. Half the success in building a solid dating relationship that can blossom into an awesome marriage is finding the right person.

DISCERNING CHARACTER

This final chapter could be summed up with one phrase: Dating is discernment. Our premise is that the dating experience is about being able to discern who this person really is. *Webster's Collegiate Dictionary* expresses this idea perfectly: Discernment is "the quality of being able to grasp and comprehend what is obscure . . . a searching that goes beyond the obvious or superficial." Think about it. That's precisely the goal of dating.

Here's why: the people you go out with are *marketing gurus*. They are always on their best behavior, always putting their best foot forward. Women, in particular, are masters. They call it "makeup." Hellooo! The very name says it all, and they don't stop with the billion-dollar cosmetic industry's wares. Somehow they learn how stripes make them look shorter, taller, thinner, or fatter, as needed. This outfit provokes this response, this fragrance elicits that reaction. And so it goes.

Make no mistake, men and women will focus primarily on impressing you. Their aim is to portray themselves as charming, polite, polished, and attractive. They will tell you what you want to hear and behave in ways that they believe you would want to see. One person put it like this, "As a single person, I feel like I'm always on display. I have to constantly be on guard for fear of running into someone who could be a potential date. I don't want to miss the right one." Let's face it, if you've been trying to land a date with that certain woman who likes the ballet, guess what? Suddenly, your idol is Barishnikov and you're telling people you always wanted to be a dancer. You start speaking in Russian and wearing tights beneath your blue jeans. You love the ballet! If you think about it, the dating practices of our culture are quite bizarre (i.e., the emphasis on hiding your true self). In other cultures, the parents play a primary role in picking out marriage partners, and the game playing is kept to a minimum. While we could certainly benefit from adapting some practices of other cultures, we aren't interested in telling you to "kiss dating good-bye" as some have suggested. So, we're stuck with the tremendous challenge to get beyond the masks and discover the true person underneath. Your job is to penetrate this natural tendency to impress and gain insight into who they *really* are. Ultimately, you're trying to discern character.

WHAT IS CHARACTER?

If you could strip away the physical attributes, the clothes, the polite sayings, even the charming personality, everything that remains comprises character. It is basically who you are on the inside. Character entails our convictions (not briefly and lightly held opinions), principles, and moral integrity that guide our behavior. In other words, character is who we really are and how we really act, not the ideals we market to the world. Others have referred to character as simply who you are when no one is looking. Because of our culture's emphasis on style over substance, character, by its very nature, cannot be perceived very quickly. The task of discerning character is a long-term process. You can't expect to know one's insides really without spending long periods of time with that person in many different settings and under many circumstances.

Getting beyond the superficial qualities is to consider what you need in a mate—the essential inner qualities that make or break a healthy, successful relationship. We want you to be able to look past the superficial and discern whether or not your partner has the inner goods necessary to sustain a healthy relationship. We have identified five *essential character qualities* (ECQs) that you need in a mate: faithful, honest, committed, forgiving, and giving. You will find these to be extremely obvious and yet so often overlooked. Let's take a closer look at these qualities.

1. Faithful

A faithful person is loyal and can demonstrate an allegiance to others. As you observe this person in his social relationships or business practices does he pass the test of loyalty? Is this someone who keeps her promises? Does this person have the capacity for fidelity? Have there been past incidences of infidelity or disloyalty in former relationships?

Many relationships start out of a sense of disloyalty to another. I (Ben) remember Sandy, an outgoing woman in her mid-thirties. She was so proud and excited to tell me about her new boyfriend, Fred. I must admit, when she described him it sounded like he was quite a catch. He seemed to have all the right moves, to say all the right things; it appeared that he really loved Sandy. The only problem was that Fred was married. But she rationalized that Fred didn't love his wife and was in the process of separating from her. As I discussed my concerns with her, Sandy seemed to have some rationalization for everything about this relationship. As we ended the session, I asked her to find out how Fred and his wife first got together. Well maybe it was a lucky guess, but eventually Sandy discovered that Fred had begun his relationship with his current wife the same way he began his relationship with Sandy—out of disloyalty. We discussed this as a pattern, and explored the probability that Fred would continue to do this. I asked her, "What makes you think you are different from all the rest?" If Fred was disloyal to others, why would Sandy be different? Never continue a relationship with someone out of unfaithfulness unless you are willing to deal with heavy consequences.

2. Honest

An honest person is genuine, and free of deception. This quality of honesty encompasses three aspects: words, actions, and personhood. First, it has to do with his word. Can you trust him to tell you the truth? Does he mean what he says? Is he prone to lies or deception (even "white" lies)? Second, honesty involves actions and behavior. Does he conduct daily behavior in an upright manner? Do others consider him to be credible, reputable, and respectable? Finally, does he have the capacity to be real, genuine, and transparent? How difficult is it to know this person? Are you able to discern his inner qualities over a period of time, or does this person have so many layers of defenses and disguises that you cannot penetrate?

Laura came in to see me (Sam) three months after her honeymoon. She was distraught over her lack of connection with her husband. Her specific complaint was, "He won't open up to me. He's so secretive. He's always traveling, and he claims to be engaged in complex business deals." She further revealed that he wouldn't tell her anything else about his business practices ("it was too complicated"). After we discussed the history of their relationship, it was clear that she was initially attracted to her husband for the same reasons that she was now upset. She admitted that she was drawn to him in the beginning because he was the "strong, silent type." She was also intrigued by his "mysterious" nature. In reality, she was attracted to him because he was withdrawn and hard to figure out. Go figure! If you are drawn to someone for that kind of reason, you may be asking for trouble.

3. Committed

The idea here is to find someone who can demonstrate a lifestyle of commitment, not someone who just verbalizes his commitment. Anybody can say, "Yes, I'm committed to you." But do they have what it takes to be committed to the relationship for the long haul? Dr. James Dobson speaks of two kinds of commitment: Contract Commitment and Covenant Commitment. Contract Commitment is like a business agreement—if you fulfill your obligations, I'll fulfill mine. If you should violate the agreement, then I have a way out, an escape clause. This form of commitment is conditional (might as well get an attorney to draw up a marriage contract). Sadly, this seems to be the typical attitude in our society today.

On the other hand, a Covenant Commitment is one that emphasizes an agreement to fulfill my end of the deal, regardless of your participation. It is an unconditional agreement to hang in for life. *In fact, God has a kind of covenant relationship with all Christians. Regardless of our behavior or irresponsibility, He is committed to fulfilling His end of the agreement.* He will never leave us or forsake us, He promises eternal salvation, and He provides unconditional love and acceptance.[2]

Susan worked in the legal profession and was used to giving politically correct answers (which are often no answers at all).

I'll (Sam) never forget our first pre marital counseling session. When I asked Susan about her commitment to Charles, she responded, "Well, sure I'm committed because I'm in love with him." She went on to confess, "But if something happened, and we sort of fell out of love, and depending on how we feel at the time, there is always that possibility that something unforeseen could happen." You get the picture. Susan represents someone with contract commitment. She has conditionality written all over her. True love is an unconditional commitment to an imperfect person. That's the best definition of love we know of. That *is* love. However, at a gut level some of you may be saying that sounds too ideal, too high a standard. Some wise woman once proclaimed, "When I looked at my groom during the wedding ceremony, I suddenly realized that I couldn't honestly promise to love him perfectly. But *I could promise never to quit.*" Similarly, Dr. Dobson expresses the ultimate secret for lifelong love: "If you choose to marry, enter into that covenant with the resolve to remain committed to each other for life."[3] We agree with Dobson.

4. Forgiving

Forgiveness is simply releasing a person from the debt you perceive they owe you. It is about letting go of the need to punish, resent, or hold grudges when you have been wronged. When we find couples who have been happily married for thirty-five or forty years, we often ask them to sum up the secret to their success. Of course, people give many different answers ranging from "A lot of hard work and commitment" to "A lot of play and a good sense of humor." But almost always one of the reasons given is "the ability to forgive each other." If you are serious about finding someone with the character trait of forgiveness, make sure they know about the ten magic words: "*I am sorry,*

I was wrong, will you forgive me?" If you don't know why these words possess a little bit of magic, go try them out for yourself. What kind of person are you dating? Is he quick to condemn and slow to release others off the hook? Does he hold grudges or resentment? How does he resolve conflicts? Do you see an eagerness to compromise, let go, and move forward? Is there evidence of a forgiving spirit? We hope so. A successful relationship between two imperfect people must be bathed in an atmosphere of daily, mutual forgiveness.

5. Giving

This quality is not about giving material gifts but, rather, the capacity for selfless behavior. Giving means putting others first. A giver gets outside of himself and gives to you rather than always seeking to get from you. Such a person has the capacity to be "other-centered." He can demonstrate sensitivity to your needs and the ability to meet those needs. Most importantly, a giver desires to see you grow and to love you in a way that promotes wholeness. When the romantic love fades (which indeed it will), a relationship can be sustained only by a deeper kind of love, the kind that seeks to see you grow.

Steve was the opposite of a giver; not only was he self-absorbed, but he actually thought he was a humble, selfless, giving person! His ability to perceive himself accurately was incredibly poor. He constantly whined about his aches and pains, pestering his girlfriend to give him back rubs and foot rubs. Each day brought fresh incidences of discomfort at work that required Donna's attention. Donna was happy to bless her boyfriend, but after a while she noticed the one-way giving pattern and punted him. Over time she saw his true character and spared herself a lifetime of misery.

Helpful Hints for Discerning Character

1. *Crisis reveals someone's true character.* When someone is faced with a difficult circumstance or crisis situation, he usually doesn't have time to think. At crucial moments when a sudden decision must be made, people do what comes natural. They respond from the heart. Pay close attention to people under pressure or in crisis situations if you want to know their true colors.

2. *Character is who you are when no one is looking.* If this is true, then it is vital that you place a heavy emphasis on your partner's behavior when you are together, alone and behind closed doors. The spirit of this truth suggests that the way you are treated by your partner in private is far more important than how you are treated in public, particularly around family and friends. Many can fake character in public and some are fabulous actors when the occasion calls for it. Relatedly, if you find yourself being treated in a manner that is inappropriate or disrespectful in public (when your partner is supposed to be on "best behavior"), what does this say about this person's true character? You can bet it's even worse.

3. *Friends are a window into a person's character.* To really know someone take a look at his friends. What kind of people does he hang out with? With whom does he surround himself? We all tend to gravitate toward those with whom we feel we have a lot in common. Furthermore, we usually become like those with whom we associate. Consider what the apostle Paul says in 1 Corinthians 15:33, "Do not be misled: 'Bad company corrupts good character.'" Rarely does the influence occur the other way around.

4. *Look back on prior relationships to determine patterns of behavior.* Consider whether there is a pattern of disloyalty, dishonesty, or unforgiveness in past relationships. Pay attention

to how your partner talks about his or her ex-boyfriend or girl-friend. Also, ask yourself how your partner treated his parents while growing up as well as how he treats them now. Often this will give you clues as to who a person really is. In the final analysis, behavior patterns reveal more than words or promises.

5. *Give it lots of time.* One of the points we have continued to stress throughout is the need to give yourself a lot of time in order to discover who your partner truly is. It's such an obvious truth and yet so difficult to do. It would be hard to exaggerate the importance of this truth. In fact, we devoted a whole chapter to this matter (Commandment Four, "Thou Shalt Take It Slow").

IT'S YOUR CHOICE

In the conclusion of the movie *Indiana Jones and the Last Crusade*, Donovan had "chosen poorly" in his quest for the grail, and it was finally Indiana's turn to make a choice from the many chalices set before him. Remember, he bypassed the shiny, ornate, and richly adorned goblets—those that were initially pleasing to the eye. Instead, he chose a simple, worn, and nondescript cup that, when dipped into the water to fill, revealed itself to be solid gold. Indiana drank of the cup, and the knight affirmed, "You chose *wisely*." Don't miss the point. We're not saying that you need to find someone with tarnished looks and a dusty personality. Rather, seek to be discriminating about character. Don't compromise in this crucial area. If there is ever a time to be picky, when it comes to considering your partner, this is it! All of these qualities should be *non-negotiable*. Too often we see individuals who are willing to compromise and accept three or four out of five of these qualities.

These odds sound good in Las Vegas but don't hold up to the necessary requirements for a healthy marital relationship.

Most, if not all, of the pop songs played on the radio imply that all you need is love. This directly violates the Law of Choosing Wisely. The subtle message is, "Don't be discriminating; just be glad you've got someone who loves you. Don't worry about someone's past or what is on the inside—that's all irrelevant as long as they love you." What a joke! The only way to choose wisely is to make choices based upon character—those intangible qualities. It's okay to have your "wish list" of characteristics you want in a mate, but make sure your primary focus is on what you need—good character. Here's the bottom line. When discerning character, ask yourself five simple questions:

1. Can he or she demonstrate loyalty?
2. Can he or she be open and real?
3. Can he or she hang in when the going gets tough?
4. Can he or she let you off the hook?
5. Can he or she put you first?

CONSEQUENCES OF BREAKING THIS COMMANDMENT

- You may wind up with someone who is attractive, rich, and funny, but you will be unhappy and unfulfilled because he or she isn't what you really need in a mate.

- You may settle for the first available warm body and experience the most lonely feeling of all, to be "eternally" committed to a person you don't love.

- You may live through the pain and brokenness of a relationship that has gone asunder all because you chose to become involved with the wrong person. You married someone who is lazy, dishonest, unfaithful, or spiritually uncommitted.

BENEFITS OF KEEPING THIS COMMANDMENT

- You will greatly increase your odds of getting what you want.

- You will greatly improve your chances of being in a healthy relationship.

- You will be able to discard undesirable partners early on in the dating process, thus saving time, energy, and money.

- You will become a chooser instead of a beggar in the dating game.

HELP FOR YOU WHO HAVE BROKEN THIS COMMANDMENT

- If you are currently in a relationship and you know this is not what you need or want, then get out of the relationship now. Assume that nothing will change this person. If you kiss a toad, you simply get slime in your mouth.

- If you are not attached, dating, or even "hanging out" with anyone in particular, then make a commitment to look for ECQs in your next relationship.

Conclusion

тнou sнaLt take actιon (тне eLeventн commandment)

In a country where the divorce rate is now *more* than 50 percent, the odds suggest you are more likely to have an unsuccessful marriage relationship than a successful one. For most people, the shadow of this reality provides a pretty pessimistic outlook. Sadly, the majority of singles we talk with are hesitant, tentative, and insecure about their ability to beat the odds. That's why we wrote this book! We think you can do much better than just cross your fingers and wish for the best. Our ultimate goal was to provide you with a greater sense of security and hope. We believe that you can significantly increase the odds of having an enduring marriage by following these ten simple commandments.

You were drawn to this book for a reason. Obviously, you want God's best for your dating life, and ultimately you desire a healthy love relationship. We anticipate that any truths that you may have found relevant to your experience will require some level of change. However, there is nothing worse than reading this book, agreeing with its premise and principles, and yet doing nothing about it.

If you haven't figured it out yet, we are both very action oriented. We believe that any change in one's life must be accompanied by action (literally, physical movement). Having the insight alone is just not enough. There must be a point at which you begin to "move your feet" regardless of whether or not you feel like doing so. Michele Weiner-Davis put it well when she indicated that at some point you have to stop talking to your friends and family, stop listening to tapes on self-actualization, stop reading self-help books, and begin living. The difference between those who turn their life around and live their dreams, and those who make no change is summed up in one word: *action*.[1]

As such, we would like to offer several clear-cut methods for taking action now and getting the most out of this material. If you want to gain the most benefit from this book then you must identify which laws you are violating, then take action. It may require you to break up with a partner you have been in a relationship with, because you know he or she isn't right for you. It may be that you are plagued by low self-esteem or self-doubt, and it is finally time to do something about it. Or you may have identified poor communication and conflict resolution skills, and therefore need to schedule time to learn new, healthy ways of relating. Any of these steps may be difficult or even risky—but necessary. Do you need to make changes? Are you ready to take action? Then take our advice below.

Take a Look at Yourself

It all starts with you. No one else can make you happy, whole, or complete. You must be solid and complete all by yourself. Do you know who you are? Do you feel good about yourself? Do you have a solid sense of worth and value? The answer is either yes or no! If *yes*, then forge ahead and take a look at these next considerations. If you answered *no*, then take deliberate action now! Do something about it. It's that simple. Make it your number-one goal to solidify your identity, and deal with this once and for all. Whether you do this through pastoral counseling, professional counseling, or some other avenue for growth, make it happen today.

Take Responsibility for Your Relationships

If you are the type who constantly finds yourself in unhealthy relationships, it is time to identify the patterns and resolve to change it. You don't have to be a victim of "bad luck" anymore. It's time to take responsibility for poor dating habits. Quit blaming others, and learn to avoid certain patterns and unhealthy partners. It's your choice.

Take Back What You Lost

There is yet another group who have been devastated or wounded due to repeated violations of one or a combination of commandments. For example, we have all succumbed to the temptation of going too fast in a relationship. It's easy to speed when you are excited about someone. At one time or another, we have all been guilty of putting too much emphasis on the romantic/passionate aspect of a relationship (i.e., failed to use our brain). Most of us can relate to the regrets associated with sexual indiscretion. Going too far, too soon, is all too common.

Look, we've all been there. We have all fallen in one of these crucial areas. Perhaps you have lost your confidence, dignity, or self-respect. Well, it's time to take back what you may have lost. It is up to you to start the process of healing through acknowledgment, confession, and renewal.

Take a Look Around You

Almost certainly, there are those reading this book who have a sparse dating life. You have either questioned yourself, or almost given up hope altogether. You may be wondering, "Where do you meet people these days?" Or you might have even concluded that, "All the good ones are already taken." Not so. More than likely Mr. or Ms. Right is someone you already know. The vast majority of happy, successful couples meet their partners in ordinary places as they go about their routine of everyday living. Or they meet them through close friends. In other words, it's not the bar scene, social clubs, or dating services that bring people together for a lasting relationship. It's quite possible that your future spouse is right under your nose!

Take Time Out

Whenever you find yourself in a serious relationship, you must take time out to consider the fruit of that relationship—especially when you have questions about the relationship. Above all else, there is one test that can help you determine whether or not the relationship has potential. One simple question: *Do I feel encouraged, affirmed, inspired, and challenged to grow and be a better person when I am with him or her?* That's it. Once again, if the answer is no, then it is time to take action.

Take These Laws Seriously

Finally, we want you to remember that these laws are not recommendations or suggestions. Ignore them and you pay the consequences; we can't always predict or pinpoint a direct result, but we can guarantee it will be negative. Conversely, seek to follow these laws, and you will experience positive results—blessings! Relationships don't have to be as complicated and mysterious as we sometimes make them. Obey the Ten Commandments of Dating and you shall experience clarity, security, hope, and—most of all—blessing.

Notes

Commandment 1

1. Peter Kreeft, *Knowing the God Who Loves You* (Ann Arbor, Mich.: Servant Publications, 1988), 171.
2. Rick Warren, Encouraging Word, tape ministry (Mission Viejo, Calif.).
3. *How the Grinch Stole Christmas*, Dr. Seuss, 1966, Turner Entertainment Company on Warner Home Video.
4. Leo Buscaglia, *Living, Loving, and Learning* (Ballantine, 1983).

Commandment 3

1. C. E. Rollins, *Are We Compatible?* (Nashville: Thomas Nelson, 1995), 1.

Commandment 4

1. *Heart & Stroke Statistical Update*, American Heart Association, Inc. 1998, Available from http://www.amhrt.org/Internet.
2. Divorce statistics acquired from the Census Bureau, 1995.

3. Neil Clark Warren, *Finding the Love of Your Life* (Colorado Springs: Focus on the Family, 1992), 9.

4. Dr. James Dobson, Focus on the Family newsletter, provided the basis for this premise.

5. Dr. JamesDobson, *Life on the Edge* (Dallas: Word,1995), 112.

Commandment 6

1. John Harris, "Why Wait?" presentation, seminar notes, Campus Crusade for Christ (March 1991).

2. Ibid.

3. Carolyn See, "The New Chastity," *Cosmopolitan*, Nov. 1985, 382.

4. Rick Stedman, *Pure Joy—The Positive Side of Single Sexuality* (Chicago: Moody Press, 1993), 59–60.

Commandment 7

1. *Spin* Magazine/NBC News Poll, 1996.

2. Rosanne Rosen, *The Living Together Trap* (Far Hills, N.J.: New Horizon Press, 1993), 2.

3. Harold Ivan Smith, *Singles Ask* (Minneapolis: Augsburg Press, 1998), 145.

4. Barbara Vobejda, "Number of Couples 'Cohabitating' Soaring as Mores Relax," *Houston Chronicle* (5 December 1996), 13A.

5. William R. Mattox Jr., "Nag, Nag, Nag," *Focus on the Family Magazine*, 1996.

6. Rosen, *The Living Together Trap*, 82.

7. Roger Hillerstrom, *Intimate Deception* (Portland, Oreg: Multnomah Press, 1989), 29.

8. Stedman, *Pure Joy*, 166.

Commandment 8

1. John Gottman, *From the Roots Up: A Research Based Marital Therapy Workshop*. Seminar notes given in Dallas in February 1997.

2. Howard Markman, Scott Stanley, and Susan Blumberg, *Fighting for Your Marriage* (San Francisco: Jossey-Bass, Inc., 1994), 6.

3. Stephen R. Covey, *The Seven Habits of Highly Effective People* (New York: Simon & Schuster, 1989), 253.

Commandment 10

1. Henry Cloud, *Single Connection* interview with Ben Young, (Winning Walk Ministries, October, 1996).

2. Dr. James Dobson, Focus on the Family Radio interview, June 1998.

3. Dr. James Dobson *Life on the Edge*, 104.

Conclusion

1. Michel Weiner-Davis, *Change Your Life and Everyone in It* (New York: Simon & Schuster, 1995), 53.

About the Authors

Ben Young currently directs one of the largest singles ministries in the United States. In the ten years he has been on the staff at Second Baptist Church in Houston, Texas, he has seen the singles program more than double to its current size of 7,200. He holds a Masters of Divinity from Southwestern Baptist Theological Seminary. Ben also hosts *The Singles Connection*, a nationally syndicated radio talk show exclusively for singles. Ben is a popular speaker at conferences and retreats throughout the country.

Sam Adams, Psy. D., is a licensed clinical psychologist. He earned his bachelor's degree from Baylor University. He went on to receive his master's from Western Seminary and a doctorate from George Fox College Graduate School of Clinical Psychology. He currently maintains a full-time counseling practice in Austin, Texas, where his primary emphasis is on relationship and marital issues. He resides in Austin with his wife, Julie, and their three children.

for speaking engagements and conference information:

Ben Young
Single Life Ministries
6400 Woodway
Houston, TX 77057
713.465.3408

Dr. Sam Adams
5524 Bee Caves Road
Building E, Suite 1
Austin, TX 78746
512.328.9700

or you may check out the Single Connection web site at singleconnection.org.

also available

The Ten Commandments of Dating video kit for use in small group study, youth training, and weekend retreats. This kit includes one video that contains four fifteen-minute sessions, an audio instruction tape for the group leader, and a study guide.
ISBN: 0-7852-9619-0
Price: $39.99